TIME
SHIFTS

"Von Braschler is back with THE book the paranormal world has been waiting for! Braschler walks us through a world of possibilities and tests the paradigms of what we think we know while examining what mysteries of our human experience are still waiting to be revealed."

DAVE SCHRADER, HOST OF *DARKNESS RADIO* AND
TRAVEL CHANNEL'S *THE HOLZER FILES*

"*Time Shifts* is a remarkable book, full of thought-provoking stories, fascinating information on how time travel works, and valuable exercises to help you experiment with alternate realities. Like all of Von Braschler's books, *Time Shifts* is well researched and contains a wealth of practical information. Highly recommended."

RICHARD WEBSTER, AUTHOR OF
LLEWELLYN'S COMPLETE BOOK OF DIVINATION

"More people should step out of their black-and-white world and dare to explore the gray areas. That's where the adventures begin. Time slips and time travel are real, and crossing the threshold between what was, the now, and the upcoming are experiences we are all capable of. Von Braschler's *Time Shifts* is a wonderfully interesting and informative way to understand time travel and learn how to break the barriers and experience time shifts first-hand. Passports are not required."

MARLA BROOKS, HOST OF *STIRRING THE CAULDRON*
PODCAST ON PARA-X RADIO NETWORK
AND AUTHOR OF *WORKPLACE SPELLS*

"Fascinating book. *Time Shifts* provides specific exercises that can teach readers how to experience this 'time shift' or 'quick switch.' Highly recommended."

ALBERT AMOA SORIA, PH.D., AUTHOR OF
AWAKEN THE POWER WITHIN

TIME SHIFTS

EXPERIENCES OF SLIPPING INTO THE PAST AND FUTURE

VON BRASCHLER

Destiny Books
Rochester, Vermont

Destiny Books
One Park Street
Rochester, Vermont 05767
www.DestinyBooks.com

Text stock is SFI certified

Destiny Books is a division of Inner Traditions International

Cataloging-in-Publication Data for this title is available from the Library of Congress

ISBN 978-1-64411-239-7 (print)
ISBN 978-1-64411-240-3 (ebook)

Printed and bound in the United States by Lake Book Manufacturing, Inc. The text stock is SFI certified. The Sustainable Forestry Initiative® program promotes sustainable forest management.

10 9 8 7 6 5 4 3 2 1

Text design and layout by Priscilla Baker
This book was typeset in Garamond Premier Pro with Gotham and Supermolot Condensed used as display typefaces

To send correspondence to the author of this book, mail a first-class letter to the author c/o Inner Traditions • Bear & Company, One Park Street, Rochester, VT 05767, and we will forward the communication.

Contents

Foreword

In early spring 1990, Larry Miller and his wife, Claire, were driving from Alsip, a South Chicago suburb, to visit relatives in New Mexico. While traveling through a southwestern area of Missouri, they discovered that Interstate 44 was closed, so Larry exited an off-ramp, following signs to a detour. The midafternoon was clear, and the Millers enjoyed their unhurried ride over rolling countryside and broad pastureland. Perhaps fifteen minutes after leaving the expressway they arrived at a charming town with small shops and a friendly looking diner, like the one in the famous Edward Hopper painting *Night Hawks*. It featured big glass windows and a quietly inviting atmosphere. On the street, traffic was light, the sidewalks not crowded. A young redheaded woman was pushing a baby buggy around the park, and some kids were playing hopscotch there. There was little other activity.

The main square was dominated by an attractive vintage city hall building that appeared well preserved. It featured a tall brick clock tower. It had apparently been constructed sometime during the late 1800s. Today it appears surrounded by a broad, well-manicured public park. Claire observed that the big illuminated clock face with Roman numerals showed the wrong time. Its Victorian hands had stopped at 1:30, whereas her watch read 3:00. After pausing momentarily at a few stoplights, the Millers drove out of town and were back on the road, headed toward the detour. Or so they assumed. As before, they went speeding across the indistinguishably repetitive landscape of endless farmlands. Again the posted speed limit dropped as they approached another small town. It seemed remarkably similar to the one they had left behind only ten minutes earlier.

"All these places look alike," Larry said with a trace of boredom. But as they arrived at the town center, on the left they passed the very same diner with its big glass windows and the same few customers. Still more surprising, the old town square with its high brick clock tower stood as before on their right.

"How about that?" Larry observed. "They made an exact duplicate of that other place we came through!"

"Yeah," Claire agreed uncertainly. "But the clock is different here. In the other town, it said 1:30. Here, it's 1:00." Before her husband could respond, she exclaimed, "This *is* the same town! You must have driven in a circle. Look! There's that same lady pushing a stroller and those kids playing in the park we saw last time."

Larry was confused. "But how can that be? We drove in a straight line."

"It just *seemed* that way. Pay more attention to the road next time," she scolded him.

As before, they followed the main street out of town, this time in silence. Larry was careful this time, never missing a road sign. He conscientiously avoided all turns and followed a posted detour back to Interstate 44. About ten minutes later, the speed limit dropped again at the approach to another town.

"It's not possible," Larry almost shouted as he pulled over to a curb in the same town they'd passed through twice before. Claire crouched in grim silence, gazing out her window at the all too familiar street while her husband intently consulted a road map. "Maybe we should ask somebody," he suggested.

"No!" she insisted. "Let's just get out of here!"

Larry pulled out into light traffic. Almost immediately, the classic diner occupied by the same customers reappeared on their left, followed shortly thereafter by the main square with its old public building. The red-haired woman was still walking around the park behind her baby buggy while the same children hopscotched as before.

But when Claire looked up at the clock tower, she screamed. It read 12:30. With every pass they made through town, all of its details had been identically repeated, save for the clock face. Each time it showed a time precisely thirty minutes earlier. "Let's get out of here!" she pleaded again, now on the verge of tears. "I'm scared! I'm real scared. Go! Go! Just go!"

Unnerved, Larry put the pedal to the metal. Their car raced through the last two stoplights, luckily avoiding any collisions. Out of town and on the open road again, Larry did not let up on the accelerator. While endeavoring to keep his speeding car under control, he tried to calm his wife. She was shuddering and weeping, but he soon ran out of words. His chest seemed to tighten with growing panic, and his breath came hard and fast. But his anxiety began to slowly subside the greater the distance he put between themselves and the town.

"Claire," he finally said with a self-assurance he actually lacked, "we've been driving about eighty miles an hour for more than fifteen minutes. We should have arrived back at that town by now, but we're still on the road." She stopped crying long enough to look uncertainly at the uniformly similar farmlands blurring past her window. Maybe her husband was right.

But no! Suddenly there appeared the same signs, the same town. Larry slowed down only enough to maneuver through the two-lane streets and miss hitting anyone. He was still doing fifty in thirty-five-mph zones.

Within moments, the glassy restaurant containing its same diners was on their left again. The park's red-haired mother and baby buggy and hopscotching kids had not changed. Only the high brick clock tower was different. Both of its immense black hands pointed straight up to high noon.

As the careening car sped by the park, the brazen lungs of the old clock rang out like a doomsday toll seemingly directed at Larry and Claire. It called after them as they lurched at top speed out of town. Both Larry and his wife were filling the inside of their car with screams.

Larry did not care who or what he might crash into. A collision would at least terminate this endless horror. His speedometer passed one hundred miles per hour, while the ominous echoes of the big clock faded by degrees in the distance. Larry was determined to fly through the town at full speed next time. Hatred for whatever it was that had so terrified them had unhinged his rational mind.

But soon the environment seemed different. The countryside was not precisely the same as before. Unfamiliar farmhouses appeared on either side of the road. Larry slowed down to the fifty-five-mph speed limit. Suddenly, there was a posted sign announcing the end of the detour. Another one pointed toward Interstate 44. He pulled over to the side of the road and switched off the engine, then took Claire in his arms.

"I don't know what happened," he consoled her, "but it's over." While their powerful experience was something neither would ever forget, neither could they later recall the name of the strange town, even after examining a detailed road map of their otherwise uneventful travels through southwestern Missouri. Not surprisingly, they took an alternate route on their return trip to Illinois.

The forgoing incident was told to me by Mr. Miller himself, my former employer. He is known as a no-nonsense businessman, and he never discussed his encounter with anyone else. He had nothing to gain by sharing it with me and showed no further interest in anything paranormal. His wife, Claire, emphatically backed up his account word for word.

A similar report of time travel involves a father and his seven-year-old son who attended a Civil War reenactment at Gettysburg, Pennsylvania, during the summer of 2001. Frederick Catalano and Fred Jr. were thrilled to see hundreds of men and women dressed in authentic period costume regalia at the very location of a great event in American history. There was a re-creation of the famous battle with military bands, booming cannons, charging horse soldiers, volleys of smoking muskets, and troops in blue and gray marching under colorful banners.

After the commemorative confrontation, Frederick and Freddy joined thousands of other onlookers in numerous stalls that had been set up to display Civil War–era memorabilia. These stalls were adjacent to a rather primitive and large grandstand draped with red, white, and blue bunting. At the center of this structure, the day's reenactment continued with a tall, lanky actor whose job it was to portray Abraham Lincoln delivering the Gettysburg Address to a sizable crowd of soldiers and civilians attired in authentic-looking mid-nineteenth-century dress.

Frederick and Junior joined them to hear the well-known words recited in a Midwestern twang by the gaunt "president" and then enthusiastically applauded along with others in the audience. Afterward, members of the audience gathered around "Mr. Lincoln" to heartily congratulate him as he sat wearily at an outdoor table. Carrying the boy in his arms, Fred made his way through the press of well-wishers: "See? That's the man who led the Union during the Civil War."

"Lincoln" looked up at the father and son with a sudden, bright smile. "What's your name, little man?"

"Fweddy," the lad piped up, and the nation's sixteenth chief executive laughed, then reached up to shake his hand. "Pleasure to meet you, Fweddy! My name's Abe."

Getting into the spirit of the occasion, the elder Catalano asked, "How's the war going, Mr. President?"

At these words, the actor fell back into character. "I fear it will never end," he sighed authentically. Before he could explain he was hustled away by a "general." The crowd began to melt away.

Fred took his son to visit a few other booths before the grounds were closed. As they were leaving the park they were approached by an organizer of the event, who was also an old friend. "How'd you like the presentation, Fred?" he asked.

"Oh, it was great! Everybody played their roles so realistically, except for the guy reading the Gettysburg Address. He just didn't look very much like any of the old photos I've seen of Abraham Lincoln. The actor was tall enough but seemed too old for the part."

The organizer stopped in his tracks. "What are you talking about? We didn't have anybody reading the Gettysburg Address or portraying Lincoln at the reenactment!"

Fred described in detail the large, apparently improvised grandstand with its patriotic bunting surrounded by a crowd of listeners in blue uniforms, top hats, and gingham dresses. "Nope," the organizer insisted, "nothing even remotely like that was staged this year. I know everything that goes on here. It's my job. Look at your program. It lists all the events and facilities. No mention of Lincoln making the Gettysburg Address at a grandstand or any place else. What you saw must have been a ghost."

But Mr. Catalano's experience seemed like something other than that. His interaction with the president and the solid physicality of the entire incident was unlike any alleged haunting. Instead, he believes that he and his son inadvertently stepped back in time and into an event originally aimed at re-creating the same long-gone era—one conjuring the other in a kind of kindred frequency of similar vibrations generated by two sets of sympathetic actions occurring in the same environment.

Why the organizer and thousands of other visitors to Gettysburg that day did not share Mr. Catalano's time slip is unknown, except for speculation that only he and his son were somehow psychologically disposed to it in the same way individuals with normal vision are able to see colors that people with monochromatic vision cannot.

This experience and others like it cannot be validated by repeatable testing and consequently is often dismissed as worthless hearsay by skeptics for whom the scientific method is the only standard by which credible conclusions may be ascertained. But even they admit that a sufficiently large body of anecdotal evidence may be considered well founded if it demonstrates repeating themes in the form of discernible cycles or patterns.

This is something that Von Braschler has done in his far-ranging, representative collection of related human testimony about the reality of time slips.

For the past thirty years, I have valued him as an extraordinary colleague and have been consistently enlightened by his insightful work, which culminates in *Time Shifts*.

The subject is just now beginning to attract a rapidly growing audience of professional scholars and curious students alike. They are trying to grasp the metaphysical mechanism of this temporal phenomenon that defies everyday logic but is nonetheless common enough. They can hope for no more revealing an investigation than this truly groundbreaking opus—a guidebook into the unknown and the inscrutable.

Von Braschler's intriguing, sometimes shocking, information leads us unerringly toward his powerful conclusions no less dramatically than the denouement of a bestselling novel. But this is no fantasy. Rather, as he makes abundantly clear, the other side of reality is less than a heartbeat away from our everyday world.

FRANK JOSEPH

FRANK JOSEPH was the editor in chief of *Ancient American* magazine from 1993 to 2007. He is the author of several books, including *Before Atlantis, Advanced Civilizations of Prehistoric America, The Lost Civilization of Lemuria, The Lost Treasure of King Juba, Synchronicity & You,* and *Synchronicity as Mystical Experience.* He lives in the Upper Mississippi Valley.

Little Sidesteps
Out of Time

As strange as it may sound, you've probably heard of some person or another who claims to have slipped into another time and then returned in a confused state. And perhaps you thought it was impossible and could never happen to you. This book will show you how common slips in time really are and how you could easily have experienced something like this yourself without even realizing it.

This book also will lead you through exercises to experience time slips on a controlled basis. This will make them even more meaningful for you. After all, slips in time are the way we can explore what's beyond the rigid boundaries of our mundane world. It's a likely way that our spirit journeys. It's also how we may expand our understanding.

This is the way of the shaman in a vision quest—the Native American path of spirit walking or dream walking. The shaman seeks to witness profound glimpses into the past or future, traditionally observing what the ancestors impart to them or probing the destiny that lies ahead, which they then report back to their people. In this they act the role of the prophet and, as such, are the ultimate guides who have peeked behind every bend of the road.

This is also the mission of the yoga mystic who steps outside mundane time and space. In deepest trance, the samadhi mystic leaves his physical body to journey to unknown worlds and realities to better understand the human condition. It is the quest of every serious yogi to find union in the oneness of all and unity in the journey of the spirit.

Every hero who embarks on a great journey of discovery understands this truth. The hero steps into unknown regions and loses himself (or herself) in the process. All great heroes learn to step off the path into uncertainty where *up* might become *down* and *left* may appear on the *right*. After all, no great discoveries happen on a common path riddled with deep ruts where everyone has followed the steps of others, eyes barely open.

No, the hero takes a brave leap into uncharted space and time with eyes wide open and consciously aware. And along the hero's arc of discovery, the lost soul finds itself and finds answers hidden from common view. That's the role of the hero—the brave explorer in search of hidden truth.

It was true of Odysseus, who slayed mythical monsters and dueled with gods in worlds that most people never see. It was true of Arjuna, the hero in the Bhagavad Gita, who rode his chariot with the lord as his guide and counselor during a war.

All of us can become the hero of our own life journey because living is a process that is meant to be filled with adventure and discovery. It's a journey where you are pitted against obstacles and forced to make choices. How you survive your hero's journey is up to you. It depends on your choices and your observations. It's how you have picked your path and found your way. What have you discovered along the way?

The journey is everything. It's much more important to you at this stage than the destination. For Arjuna on a chariot with Lord Krishna, his great success was not bringing a victorious outcome to a war but finding peace and purpose in the world. For Odysseus, reaching Ithaca to resume his throne was not his greatest victory; it was encountering many surreal obstacles along the way. If you're lucky, you will find your true self along the way—the real you outside of the illusions of our physical world with perfectly pressed clothes and manicured lawns. This is the real you, without the many masks one wears to conform to our physical norms and blend into the mundane world. It is the higher self that transcends one's physical limitations.

I believe in getting lost from time to time so as to find myself. I believe in stepping off the path and following where Spirit takes me. I have tried to do that and freely include some personal adventures that I have undergone, which are outside of normal time and space. I have included other similar encounters as faithfully as possible here in the hope that you might see a pattern in the whole.

This pattern could work for you. This won't be such a big stretch for people who have daydreamed and found themselves miles from home in a different time and place. It will not seem that odd for individuals who have experienced lucid, vivid dreams and felt certain they really *were* somewhere outside of their own memories. It will prove easy for everyone who recalls going through a normal day but then suddenly slips into another time and place where things seemed quite real—if only for an instant.

You see, all of us probably all slip in and out of time and space on a regular basis in our regular lives without much thought about it. We just shrug it off and tell ourselves how strange, that it's certainly nothing to take seriously. Most assuredly, it's something we don't talk about as a rule.

The basic truth is that our spirit longs to be free and explore. That energetic part of us that is trapped most of the time in a dense, physical body like a shroud instinctively knows how to get out. And once it gets out, it longs to experience and grow. It wants to learn and evolve.

This book offers you help in exploring and setting your spirit free.

ONE

Classic Stories of Time Shifts

Every now and then somebody reports stepping out of normal time and space. It doesn't seem to matter where they live, the time of day or year, or their background. Nobody is exactly certain how they appear to sidestep normal reality for a short time. This is because there is not enough empirical evidence from these random occurrences to study. Also, most people don't like to talk about what happened to them. Probably most people who experience these very personal time shifts feel awkward and disoriented as a result, and many of the details of the experience may be difficult to rationally analyze as the situation is outside a personal or social frame of reference.

Nonetheless, there are many anecdotal stories of these experiences, which very often are called time slips because the person slips out of normal time for a short duration. We should accurately call the time of the escape a duration because it is hard to measure by any sort of clock or watch. The one thing we do know from personal observation of people who experience these time slips is that they have little sense of ordinary time and often remark that they are surprised how much time has elapsed in the ordinary, mundane, physical world while they were "gone."

Time as it's commonly measured in this physical, three-dimensional world, of course, is an arbitrary consensus. We find it culturally convenient to agree to a 24-hour day and a 365-day year based on solar time. The way we measure things in our mundane world on a minute level tells us when we should meet each other, arrive at work, and gather for dinner.

We choose to live in a world of materialism where we reduce everything to consensus measurements. We are linear thinkers who see a starting point to everything, a midpoint, and an end line. That is what comes from living in a three-dimensional world that sees everything left to right, down to up, and front to back.

We measure things with our five physical senses and live with the self-imposed restrictions of physics in a physical world. It is like we live inside a box and cannot imagine what happens outside our box, let alone experience reality outside this box. It is a boxed-in feeling!

But Creation is bigger than that. It is unlimited without end. All of Creation, including our world and everything in it, constantly evolves and transforms into something new. Change is constant, and life is continuously evolving. And just as nature in our world goes through transformation seasonally and new life appears out of old life, the cosmos unfolds with new planets, new stars, new galaxies, and new life. It has no beginning and no end.

The present instant that you experience evolves into the next instant, and each one has the freshness of a new "now." We dream of the past that never ended, and we dream of the future that awaits our attention as we experience each moment in time as precious and pregnant with potential when we perceive it.

So maybe our idea of "then" and "later" is arbitrary, as the rational mathematician Gottfried Leibniz observed. Maybe in the unfolding universe there is one continuous, endless timeline. As such, our ability to perceive is seemingly dependent on when and where we focus our attention. Where we stand, we call "now." That is where the light is best for our observation. That's all that we see.

But what about people who seem to experience time shifts? Granted, these experiences seem rare and random. Such experiences are generally disruptive because they come outside of our normal, neat way of organizing a personal view of reality. But does that make the reality beyond these sidesteps any less valid? Do a microscope or binoculars change reality or simply give us a better view of the world outside our normal level of perception?

How else can we look outside the box?

This book examines the reality experienced by everyday people who looked outside the box without a looking glass. The first set of time travelers we will examine are part of what we sometimes call urban legends in stories that have been reported again and again as significant examples of time slips on record. I do not personally know these people but find their stories as compelling as the ones I will reveal later, which are personal encounters or secondhand stories of people I know and trust. I think the combination of these stories shows a reliable pattern that's believable and enlightening.

Charlotte Moberly, Versailles, 1901

Our first eye-popping example is the famous story of two educated ladies at Versailles. This widely reported tale involves Charlotte Moberly, president of Oxford's St. Hugh's College, and her friend Eleanor Jourdain. They were visiting the Palace of Versailles and the gardens there in 1901.

After a brief inspection of Versailles, the women left for the Trianon Palaces in the gardens. Since they found the Grand Trianon closed during their visit, they visited the Petit Trianon, a delightful building that had once served as Marie Antoinette's private palace. While inspecting the Petit Trianon, they encountered a cottage and garden. That's where their journey became a bit unusual, according to their personal account titled *An Adventure,* written in 1911.

In the garden, the women reported seeing a wide range of men dressed in various costumes from different time periods. One man with a sombrero introduced them to a passage to the palace. There Charlotte Moberly reportedly spotted a distinguished lady who was sketching a picture of the little palace. Moberly said she later identified this woman upon seeing a portrait of Marie Antoinette. The two visitors reportedly revisited Versailles several times, but things there never appeared the same as during their first encounter. They noted that the gardens had become noisy and cluttered with tourists.

Despite criticism, Moberly continued to have paranormal experiences throughout her life. Jourdain, a vicar's daughter and a professional woman, died mysteriously in 1924.

The Society for Psychical Research reviewed the book that had been written by the women of their adventure out of time. One observation was that elaborate costume parties had been organized at Versailles by French poet Robert de Montesquiou, and a bridge described by the women in their vision was discovered in an old map of the Trianon gardens. The map, found in 1903, showed a bridge that did not exist when the women had first visited there in 1901. In fact, the bridge was not listed on any other map. Clearly, the women had visited a scene from the past, if only briefly.

Their story sounds a little like ghost stories wherein spirits of deceased people appear to be living out their former lives in the costumes of their time when alive. There is a difference here, however. Haunting spirits cross timelines from the days they once lived. In time slips, living people cross space-time into another period.

Charlie Chaplin, Los Angeles, 1928

During the opening of Charlie Chaplin's 1928 movie, *The Circus,* a scene outside a theater shows a woman passing by, seemingly out of place. Because of the stir over the movie's opening, the woman attracted a lot of attention, particularly given the way she acted. People noticed that she appeared to be talking into some sort of mobile device that resembled a telephone.

This is an urban legend that people have tried to sort out for years. Some investigators have explained that the woman's device might have been an early hearing aid. The woman appeared not to listen to the device, however, but spoke into it as though engaged in a conversation.

This would appear to be a time slip. But was the woman who was speaking into the device time traveling, or were the observers who spotted her the travelers? There are a lot of little oddities about this story that seem to defy explanation. They do, however, show a pattern of sporadic slips out of time.

Icy Sedgwick, the author of many excellent books and a lively blog, collects these sorts of stories. In her blog post "Time Slips: Urban Legend, Ghost Story, or Utter Nonsense?" she tells about a man who bought three dozen envelopes for a single shilling in 1973 from a shop in Great Yarmouth, England. He purchased them from a clerk dressed in Edwardian clothing, which was obviously out of date. The man returned to the same shop a few weeks later to find someone else working there. In fact, the entire shop looked different—decidedly more modern. He learned that the business that made the envelopes he had purchased days before had stopped production fifteen years earlier.

Sedgwick continues with a story of two married couples who had a strange drive through France in 1979. They stopped at an old-fashioned inn that didn't have telephones, elevators, or modern windows. They thought it quaint and took photos. Shortly thereafter, they decided to return to this quaint inn. They could not find it, however. And when they processed their roll of film from their earlier trip, none of the photos they had taken at the old inn were included among the negatives.

Another time slip story from Sedgwick's blog involves a 1941 photo of man who appears to be wearing modern clothing that wasn't available back then. His modern sports sweater stands in stark contrast to his glasses, which look like something from the 1920s. Was he a time traveler, perhaps?

Planes in the Future, Scotland, 1935

In 1935, British Royal Air Force marshal Sir Victor Goddard was flying near Edinburgh, Scotland, when he noticed an abandoned airfield below, which appeared overgrown. It was situated in a field of old hangars with cows grazing nearby. He got some distance away from it when a storm seemed to pull him back toward the airfield.

The storm suddenly disappeared as he passed over the airfield a second time. On the second pass he said that newer, yellow planes dotted the airfield. He also saw a monoplane that he didn't recognize. Also, workers there were dressed in strange blue uniforms.

It took him years to make any sense of what he had seen. Be that as it may, years later the Scottish Air Force started painting planes yellow. The airfield then acquired the planes that he had seen. Also, the workers at the airfield indeed wore blue uniforms instead of the brown ones that Goddard was more accustomed to. This decorated pilot eventually published his experience in his book *Flight Towards Reality*.

Tara MacIsaac of the *Epoch Times* recounts some of the amazing stories of time slips that were published by the *Liverpool Echo* in England. One of the best is a story of a thief who was running from a security guard in 2006 but looked back to see that the guard was no longer behind him. Instead, he saw cars of an earlier era and people dressed in a style that had been popular decades earlier. The thief looked for a newspaper and saw a publication date of 1967. He ran down another street and found himself back in 2006, although he could look down the street where he had been and still see people and cars back in 1967.

Upon investigation, the *Echo Journal* determined that the account given by the thief was accurate down to every last detail, for he was able to describe where various shops and landmarks were located in 1967. The security guard also related that the thief seemed to vanish into thin air while he was chasing him.

The security guard had chased him down Bold Street in Liverpool, where other phantom images have been reported.

The *Echo* also included a phantom image seen by two different people in 1971. They reported seeing an eccentric inventor testing a contraption on the River Mersey. That was a well-documented event that did occur. Only it happened in 1821.

Yesterday's Prices, Liverpool, England, 2006

In a similar story related by Tara MacIsaac also in the *Epoch Times*, a young woman who entered a Liverpool shop she did not recognize. She was visiting Liverpool and wanted to buy a few things near Lord Street and Whitechapel for her mother. She found a store with extremely low prices, she felt, but the cashier and manager of the shop looked confused when she handed them her credit card for payment. They told her she needed cash, not a card. Since she didn't carry enough money on her to make her purchase, she returned without her basket of bargains.

When she told her mother this curious story, her mother insisted that the store had closed long ago to make way for a bank now situated there.

Naval Cadets Visit Medieval England, 1957

One of the best reported stories of time shifts has to be the story of three British boys in 1957 who apparently visited medieval England. The story of the three boys and their detailed account was reported by Mike Dash for *Smithsonian* magazine and elsewhere.

The three young men, all of whom were fifteen, were Royal Navy cadets in England taking part in a map-reading field test that was intended to direct them to the Suffolk village of Kersey. As they approached, the streets were deserted and they heard church bells ringing, However, the ringing stopped as soon as they entered the village. And although they walked through town looking for the church and its bell, there was no church to be seen.

They were also haunted by the songs of a bird that had faded as they approached the village. Even the wind had died down, and few leaves stirred in the trees, which cast no shadows in a normal manner.

As well, Kersey itself looked far different from what they had expected. The old-style houses, erected on high streets, were ragged and timber framed, as though built by hand. As the boys peered into these unoccupied houses, they found greenish, smeared windows. They later described the walls of the houses as having been white-washed in a crude manner. The rooms were empty and had no furniture. As well, the lads were struck by the stillness of the ducks who remained motionless on the pond. They found the entire scene out of time and very surreal.

In the future, they would describe Kersey as a ghost village that seemed to them to exude a sense of sadness and depression. They also felt a certain unfriendliness in the old village and a sense that they were somehow being watched by people they could not see. It appears that they had stepped far back in time to the earliest days of the little town. Kersey is an ancient Anglo-Saxon village, first mentioned about the year 900.

Startled by what they had seen, the boys turned and ran away. They climbed a hill and did not look back until reaching the top. Then they heard bells ringing again and saw smoke rising from chimneys, although none of the chimneys had appeared to be emitting smoke earlier. They ran again to put even more distance between themselves and the strange old village.

The young cadets were actually strangers to this part of eastern

England, and knew nothing about its features or past prior to their visit for this mapping exercise. They reported their findings to their superiors, who were skeptical about their tall tale.

At some later date, the three young cadets located Kersey on a modern map. They had found a place they could never forget; a place that didn't fit or make much sense to them.

The boys continued to discuss their strange visit to the "village out of time" for years. One of the boys contacted a leading member of the Society for Psychical Research in the late 1980s, author Andrew MacKenzie. He explored their claims extensively and discussed them in his 1997 book, *Adventures in Time*. MacKenzie noted that the boys described aspects of early-day Kersey that dated back to medieval times. The author also determined that the house one boy identified in 1957 as a butcher's shop dated back to 1350 and that it had indeed served as a butcher's shop until approximately 1790.

MacKenzie also noted that the cadets' experience in that ancient village had occurred in the summer of 1957. But it did not appear to be summer in the village when they were there.

The silence and sadness the boys sensed in medieval Kersey, he determined, would correspond in time to the Black Death that had plagued the site in the mid-fourteenth century, killing half of the population there. MacKenzie felt that the cadets might have seen the village in the aftermath of the plague.

That would explain how they had not been able to find the church and its bell, for which this village was known (although they had heard the bell ringing). The church had been only half completed during the plague. In his research, MacKenzie consulted histories of the area as well as various paintings. His findings on this elaborate sidestep into another time by three watchful cadets make this one of the most compelling stories of time slips.

One thing that seems consistent in nearly every exploration into time shifts is that there is little or no interaction with the inhabitants one encounters. People out of time do not appear as real to the people one encounters, it would seem. Inhabitants one encounters in these time slips do not seem fully conscious of time travelers in the normal sense, either. It is as though visitors to another time are like invisible witnesses and not fully engaged where they land.

One explanation, perhaps, is that one is not fully there in a physical sense but is there in an energy body or spirit body. That would seem to be true also of visions of the past that have energy but no physical body.

The Disappearing House, Oklahoma, 1971

Jason Offutt, paranormal investigator, and author of *What Lurks Beyond* and other books, relates a story under "Cases of Time Slips" online about men in a pickup truck near Poncas City, Oklahoma, in the fall of 1971. Three men in a white Ford pickup drove up to a cattle pasture there. They worked for a distributor of cattle feed and had been dispatched to this country setting to pick up a feeder.

They found something odd in their travels, however—something that left them dumbfounded for many years to come.

They opened an unlocked barbed-wire gate and entered the property it accessed. They drove onto the property with grass high over the truck's hood and passed through this high grass to a tank that was close to a red barn.

Once there, they got out of the truck. But then they realized the tank was too heavy to load, so they decided to leave. They drove around the red barn and saw a large two-story house. They said that it was a white building without lights.

The three men drove back to the cattle feed company, where the boss said he'd drain the tank so it wouldn't be too heavy to load. They then returned to the property over the path they had previously cut through the tall grass just the day before. After they loaded the tank, they pulled around the red barn as before, expecting to see the same white house again.

But they did not see the house. They inspected the place where they had seen the two-story house earlier but saw no signs of a foundation. Nor did they see any signs of a demolition having taken place. They discussed the disappearance among themselves for years but could never reach any plausible conclusion.

Rudolph Fentz, New York, 1950

The strange story of Rudolph Fentz was first told in a short story titled "I'm Scared," written by Jack Finney in the September 15, 1951, edition of *Collier's* magazine. This article, like so many descriptions of the Fentz story told subsequently, was treated on the surface as fiction, since it seems hard to swallow.

A man described by witnesses as about thirty years old and dressed conspicuously in period Victorian clothes with top hat and mutton chop sideburns appeared lost and confused in New York City traffic. He stared at cars, seemingly disoriented, and then he walked into traffic and was struck and killed.

A police investigation failed to determine his identity, although the contents of his pockets seemed oddly out of place and time. He was carrying a livery bill, a letter from Philadelphia dated 1876, old bank certificates, and old coins including one never seen before. And while he remained at the mortuary for days, nobody reported him missing. He carried a business card that read Rudolph Fentz, so it was concluded that that was probably his name.

Additional research located the widow of Rudolph Fentz Jr., who reported that her late husband told the amazing story of his father, Dr. Rudolph Fentz Sr., age twenty-nine, going out for a stroll one evening and never returning. No clues into his disappearance were found, she reported. Her father-in-law, she said, had mutton chop sideburns and was wearing a Victorian-era suit with top hat when he left the house forever that night.

While this story was initially reported as fiction, it has enjoyed a long life as urban legend. This unsolved mystery has received attention worldwide over the decades and is considered by many to be proof positive of time travel.

You be the judge.

TWO

Possible Explanations for Time Slips

Do these stories of time slips make any sense, really? While history includes a few such odd stories of people who somehow seem to sidestep ordinary time and space, we must admit that not very many people report doing so. We hear an unusual story here or there, often told reluctantly by a baffled person who is not comfortable speaking publicly for fear of being doubted and ridiculed. And people who report experiencing what we call a shift in time rarely if ever report a second encounter.

In just about all cases, time slips seem to be short diversions, although these escapes outside ordinary time and space seem to take longer than the time traveler might perceive. Long lapses sometimes occur, although the traveler senses being gone only a short amount of time. Clearly, time outside of our three-dimensional, physical world is measured very differently.

Unfortunately, it is generally hard to verify these stories. We are left to believe or disbelieve the person who makes the claim to having had the experience. There is, of course, the occasional case that involves more than a single time traveler, which adds some credence to the story. And often what they report seeing seems outside their normal frame of reference. In the case of travelers into the past, in some instances histories and pictures seem to verify their claims. Also, visions of time travelers into the future can be verified later when their visions become manifest for all to see.

If we were to evaluate these accounts outside normal time and space, we might logically examine them from various perspectives and thus offer possible explanations. Some suggestions tend to accredit the experiences, and others cast doubts on their authenticity.

Some possible criticisms of time shift claims might include the following:

1. Delusions
2. Confusion
3. Highly suggestible imagination
4. Memories of past lives
5. Psychic precognition of the future
6. Dreaming
7. Creative imagination

And some possible support for time shift claims might include the following:

1. Black holes
2. Energy vortexes
3. Raised consciousness
4. Our human ability to go outside ordinary space-time
5. Astral travel
6. Moving in the light as energy bodies
7. Holes in the fabric of our perceived reality

Admittedly, this is not a total listing of possible explanations for people who report time shifts, but it is a start. Let us consider some of the reasons against believing that these time slips really occur.

Are These Possibly Just Delusions?

People may claim that all sorts of things happened to them, but we cannot simply accept personal accounts without verification, especially without witnesses or any tangible proof. Some people making these claims might simply crave attention. Others could make things up to somehow delude themselves into believing that they experienced something out of the ordinary. Consequently, we must consider the emotional and mental stability of the person involved. Was this person feverish or on drugs? Was this person possibly hallucinating? Does this person have a history of delusions or fabrications?

This forces us to weigh the credibility of the person. We can probably diminish or disregard claims by people who have a history of delusion or gross fabrications. We might find their account of perceiving a time and place outside normal reality as curious and interesting to a point, but ultimately questionable.

But there are also claims of perceived time shifts by some very credible people who cannot be so easily dismissed in this manner. When you have two academic professionals from renowned universities who claim they saw the same thing together one afternoon, it is hard to dismiss their credibility on the grounds of delusional thinking. And the same might be said of three cadets of the Royal Navy on a disciplined field exercise together. Not only would they seem to be reliable witnesses, but they also enjoy a degree of credibility. The experience did not happen to one person alone but was simultaneously experienced by companions to better validate the event. We have all heard of mass hysteria, but naval cadets on a programmed drill and two academics on a tour would seem to be reliable people in a stable setting.

Could People Simply Be Confused?

Everyone gets confused now and then. That is possible, right? A thief is running down a dark street and gets disoriented. But then what he thinks he sees does not add up. So, he seeks out a newsstand to look at a newspaper. Maybe he is wondering where he is. Then he sees a future date on the newspaper and gets the surprise of his life. And what of the policeman chasing him who sees him temporarily vanish right in front of him? It would seem highly unlikely that both were confused in the same way and at the same time. Policemen are trained to keep their wits about them.

And what about the pilot who flies over a field of planes and airport workers from a different time? He flies over the airfield again to be certain about what he saw. Being a trained observer in the air, he looks very carefully at the strange scene on the ground to try to sort it all out. It would seem unlikely that he was simply confused for a moment.

We could say the same about the men in the pickup truck who all saw a house and then returned later to find it was no longer there. Were all these men confused? They were so certain of what they saw that they reported it to their boss. And they followed the same path through high grass trying to find the house again.

Surely, some people who think they've time traveled could be confused. Some people remember things they have seen previously in a picture, a movie, or in some other stored memory. Later, they might see something somewhat like their stored memory and try to rationalize their strange new environment with what they have already internalized as a viable reality. But that doesn't explain group encounters outside normal time and space. These sorts of stored memories tend to be personal and individualized.

Is It a Case of Highly Suggestible Imagination?

Some people, such as small children, seem able to imagine practically anything and pretend it is real. I mean, children claim to see angels in trees, right? And a lot of people these days claim that they have seen extraterrestrials. Let us not forget about people who have imaginary friends and even talk to them. Maybe they are just a little bit off their rocker. Then again, maybe children *do* see angels simply because they have fresh eyes and no conditioning *against* seeing angels.

Once again it is a matter of weighing the credibility of each report against the reliability of the witness. But we must be willing to admit that something could be a valid perception for one person even though nobody else saw it. "You just had to be there" is what these people will tell you.

Memories of Past Lives Perhaps?

It is also possible that people who claim to experience a sudden time shift are simply returning to memories of their past lives. After all, they do not seem to be interacting much with people and events when they step outside mundane space-time. And the people and events do not seem to move at a normal pace in many cases. Then again, maybe they are returning to their past lives and not just simply remembering them. If this was really your past life and there is only one timeline, with your perception limited to a physical experience of one instance along the timeline, then maybe you are simply refocusing your perception to return to another "now" on your singular timeline.

Are They a Precognition of Future Events?

People throughout time have experienced startlingly accurate precognition of future events. Sometimes we treat these people as prophets. Sometimes we call them seers or visionaries. Other times we call them dreamers. In the tradition of Native Americans and other indigenous people, a shaman is a very special person who looks into the future to determine guidance and provide a sense of direction for the tribe, which relied on the shaman's ability to do so.

Once again, when people visit their future or their past, it's a very personal journey of self-discovery on the timeline of their own extended life. In the instance of a shaman or a yogi master who claims to travel in a state of heightened consciousness along their life line as a witness of the past or future, it's a case of extending the parameters of the physical universe with its restrictive laws of physics that keep us boxed into one space and one time.

It's a matter of seeing with new eyes and hearing with new ears with heightened consciousness, something the Bible seems to advocate over and over in deploring ignorant people who have eyes yet do not see or ears yet do not hear. Clearly, this is seeing and hearing outside the box— after crawling out of the three-dimensional box of restrictive sensory perception as advocated by P. D. Ouspensky in *Tertium Origanum*. He advocated meditation to raise your consciousness to take you outside the box.

It is hard to argue with people who have precognition of future events when the events come true and match their vision, no matter how they received their vision. In any event, we must be willing to admit that they somehow attained a vantage point from which they could see the future accurately.

Are They Dreams of Past and Future Events?

That brings us to dreamers who go into some sort of state of altered consciousness with eyes shut or eyes half open to see accurate visions of another time. Dreamers often see accurate depictions of the future or detailed pictures of the past, almost as though they had been there personally. But do they go somewhere in their minds? Do they leave their physical bodies behind? And how much of them goes into the past or future as a witness? In the spiritual sciences of the East, mystics speak of the subtle energy bodies that envelop and complete our dense physical core. These energy bodies relate to other planes of reality and empower us to experience life beyond the mundane physical world that surrounds us here and now. Mystics believe that these subtle energy bodies are free to detach from the physical body and travel outside time and space. They often begin to teach students to undertake this experience by traveling in a dream body.

This might make us wonder where we really go in our most profound and vivid dreams, which seem so very real and interactive. Probably everyone has experienced dreams so realistic that they felt almost certain they really had visited another place and time. We must consider then that, if only in our consciousness, we really may have left the physical space and time where our physical body lay asleep. But what if we took our astral body, our mental body, our causal body, and our spiritual body on a journey outside of our physical body? And if we did visit another time and place, is that really time travel?

Traveling in our dreams might provide proof of time slips, but it also might offer an argument against it. Many famous cases of time shifts seem to involve people who report physically slipping into another time. But we must remember that they perceived physically being there. Since they often don't seem to interact with or observe any significant motion of others in this altered time, perhaps they were not physically present in the fullest sense but only there, as we have said before, in consciousness or in an energy body. But would that limitation make the experience of a time shift any less significant?

Are They Products of an Active Imagination?

I love the idea of an active imagination because it suggests at the get-go that one's imagination can be put into real play. Once something comes into play as part of the moving theater around us, it is an active part of our life and takes on a whole new level of perceived reality.

We imagine all sorts of things, and many of them can be verified easily by others as accurate and part of their reality as well. Just because you imagined it doesn't mean it's not real. Then again, it could be merely a figment of your imagination and totally groundless. That would likely be true of a person who could not readily process reality as most people seem to experience it.

All of these considerations should be weighed thoughtfully and subjectively when trying to evaluate whether an individual has really experienced a time shift. Let's look at some possible support for a belief in time shifts.

Black Holes?

Nobel Laureate Albert Einstein suggested that time travel might be possible by going through a black hole but that such a magical passage might prove hard to find and navigate. Black holes, apparently, are rare and a bit frightening to enter. According to Einstein, they are found in outer space beyond the physical earthly plane.

But could there be something like a black hole here in our environment? The world remains a pretty mysterious place. Also, could there be something like black holes within us that we could employ for time travel? Certainly, mysteries surround our human potential, and they're yet to be understood. Maybe we can create something like a black hole or have within us the potential to actualize one.

Energy Vortexes?

Perhaps a more likely answer would be energy vortexes, given that there are so many reports of power spots and magnetic anomalies in our world. Boats and ships occasionally disappear in the Bermuda Triangle and reappear after a strange amount of lost time. I have even experienced this myself in a small sailboat near the southeast corner of Guemes Island in the San Juan Islands off the coast of Washington. There, compasses fail you when confronted with a naturally occurring magnetic disturbance. Admittedly, I have never experienced a shift to another time while sailing there, although time does seem to pass differently on that little sailboat of mine.

I have lived near an energy vortex at a special Native American gathering place on Mount Hood in Oregon. There, odd things did happen, and visions of the past and future seemed to pop in and out. I personally observed a Native American in full feathers and a faraway look suddenly spring into view before me. I think I scared him as much as he startled me, and he quickly disappeared in front of me. I'm certain he was from an earlier time. And he probably felt that the place he saw briefly (where I was) was very futuristic. Then again, maybe he was a shaman on a vision quest.

Raised Consciousness?

For the Hindu mystic in deep meditation, or the shaman, having a heightened consciousness seems to be a requirement of traveling normal time and space. Maybe that is a key component. Maybe you must be in a certain state of mind, open to something new, including adventures off the common path.

Certainly people who don't practice deep meditation or shamanic spirit walking seem to experience time shifts, too. But maybe they reached a level of altered consciousness without the formal approach of yoga or shamanic practices. Maybe they stumbled or sidestepped into non-ordinary reality. If we could do so while dreaming, why not while *daydreaming*?

Hidden Human Potential?

Maybe it's within our unknown, latent powers to time travel all on our own. It's often said that humans utilize only about one-tenth of the brain. And beyond the brain, our consciousness connects us to all other conscious life in all Creation; we are interrelated and interdependent.

There is so much more to us than meets the eye as can be measured and weighed physically. And our human potential has yet to be fully explored.

One of the major objectives of the international Theosophical Society, a group based on Eastern spirituality and Western esoteric philosophy, is to explore the latent powers in all people. These are the inherent abilities that are virtually untapped due to our limited understanding of reality as a three-dimensional linear existence, which we attempt to measure with the restrictions of our five senses.

Astral Travel?

What if our occasional slips through time are really astral travel wherein our emotional body or body double slips outside of us and explores on its own? This could explain the doppelgänger, or etheric double, that appears like a shadowy, semi-transparent version of someone out-of-body. It is a version of you; an aspect of you.

My first teacher, the psychic author Louis Gittner, would visit people at night in an astral body they could not see. To establish that he was there, Louis decided to ring a bell in their presence, not an easy feat of astral travel, but something that an energy body could do if it gathered itself together with emotional energy, mental energy, and causal energy. Your astral double *is* an energy body, after all. When he did this with me, I was a little shocked to see him and even more shocked that he actually rang a bell to awaken me, despite warning me that he could do such a thing.

Maybe it is the astral double that slips through time. Remember the words of Einstein when he explained time as something we could travel if we could move at the speed of light. But then he warned that a physical body that travels at the speed of light would revert to pure energy. Some have considered that to be a warning that a physical body would burn up or cease to be physical in such a situation. Another way to think of it, based on Helena Blavatsky's *The Secret Doctrine* and *The Book of Dzyan*, is that a physical body could turn into an energy body and then possibly become a physical body again.

It's interesting to note that Einstein died with a worn copy of *The*

Secret Doctrine at his desk. It had handwritten notes in its margins, suggesting that he spent some time studying it. When he died, his niece asked the book's publisher, the Theosophical Society, whether they would like to receive his personalized copy of the book. The organization, founded by psychic and author H. P. Blavatsky and US Army Colonel H. S. Olcott, has maintained that science would ultimately prove basic esoteric principles, and they have other books written by Einstein in their collection. However this personal copy of one of their most important books with the physicist's handwritten notes marking key passages has special meaning for the Theosophical Society: it shows that Einstein apparently thought these ideas likely, too.

Moving in the Light?

If we were to move in the light and merge with the light, it is reasonable to assume that we would be traveling at the speed of light or time traveling. We would be entering the fast lane for certain. In such a case, we would almost certainly become light to some degree, at least during the time we were traveling.

In this I am reminded of a series of curious calls that I received years ago from a Hindu master who prescribed exercises that I should practice while meditating in the light. He told me that if I learned to properly meditate in the early morning sunlight next to running water that I could learn to live in the light and move in the light and even become the light.

Later I tried to outline these exercises for a dying friend who wanted to learn the technique and wrote about our meditations in a book titled *Moving in the Light: The Deb Bennett Story*. I discuss this entire experience later in *this* book.

The power of light was extremely meaningful to Einstein, too. He relates how he had a personal epiphany one day when he looked into the sunlight and was inspired by the infinite significance of the light. It was an *ah-ha!* moment in time that sent him rushing to his desk. Years later, his theory on the significance of light in terms of special relativity won the Nobel Prize.

Holes in the Fabric of Our Perceived Reality?

What if there were gaping holes in the fabric of our physical reality as we perceive it? What if we could accidentally or even purposely slip through one of these hidden holes on occasion?

I know that you have probably heard about energy grids on the Earth, which are not at all obvious to most of us. What if the fabric or pattern of our existence here had little gaps in it? What if you could somehow accidentally walk into one of these gaps and find yourself outside the normal grid that the rest of us routinely experience here? It makes you wonder, doesn't it?

THREE

One Confused
Twelve-Year-Old Boy

I have personally experienced time shifts, which began when I was twelve. Actually, I suspect that many people have experienced time slips without fully realizing it or allowing themselves to accept it. Eventually I was forced to accept the reality of my first sidestep into non-ordinary reality outside normal time and space, but initially I shrugged it off with confusion because I lacked the ability to grasp the situation.

It might be clear to you at this point that time shifts can be very personal and often do not seem to involve anyone else, making them hard to reconcile and accept. Most likely there is no point of reference to relate to anyone else or no point of reference in your prior experience. The lonely feeling that that engenders, I can assure you, leaves you hanging out there all by yourself in left field with a strange story that nobody around you is likely to believe. People do not simply suddenly sidestep into another time and place and then step back here, do they?

Well, I did.

The day started out without incident or warning of what was about to happen to me. I got onto a yellow school bus with other kids from my neighborhood in Everett, Washington. We weren't going to school that day but climbed aboard the converted school bus that would take us to berry fields out of town. There we spent the day playing in the dirt between rows of planted strawberries. (It might not sound like fun, but we found ways to make the day enjoyable.) Also, we could make a little pocket money spending the day out of town this way. We would pick berries for the owners of the farm, and they would pay us for our labor. Our mothers seemed glad to put us on a bus out of town under the supervision of the people who ran the berry field.

Honestly, I did not work that hard at this. My usual routine was to sing rowdy songs with my friends on the bus, pick a handful or two of berries to eat on the spot, and then disappear to the swimming hole at the river where many other pickers spent their lunch hour. I think I actually turned in a few boxes of picked berries once or twice, but mostly I just played and had fun.

The field was several miles from the town in which we lived. I didn't really know the route to the berry field for I'd never really paid attention to the roads we'd taken to get there. I just noticed that we always crossed a railroad track at its entrance.

One day at the berry field, I became extremely sick to my stomach. My friends suggested that I'd just eaten too many berries and then gone swimming on a full tummy. But I felt deep inside me that it was more serious than that. I had never felt anything like it before and really wanted to go home right then and there.

I asked the bus driver to immediately take me home, but he said that I'd have to wait to ride home with the others at the end of the day. It was only midday, however, so I searched for the field boss for some help to get home. He told me the same thing, however. I felt that I could not wait, and so I pondered how to get home on my own.

Mind you, this was before cell phones, so I could not *call* home. Nor could I call anyone I knew from the field. So, I decided I would need to find my own way home.

I looked at the entrance to the field, which was over the train tracks, and figured it was my way out of the berry patch. But I did not know what roads to take once I'd reached the entrance, which direction to go, or how long such a walk might take a twelve-year-old boy.

Then I thought about walking down the railroad tracks. I decided that they would take me back to Everett. I told my friends I was going to get home that way, but they didn't believe me. They assumed I'd just wait for the bus.

But I got onto the tracks and turned left, which I believed to be the direction of home. I envisioned how the tracks crossed right in front of my house. I did not even consider whether this was the same train track that led to my street in Everett. Train tracks, of course, make all kinds of switchbacks with various line spurs going every which way. But I got it into my fevered little brain that these tracks passed in front of my home.

So, I started walking down the tracks. The last thing I remember of the trip, however, was rounding the first curve in the track. That prevented me from looking back at the berry field I'd just left. The very next thing I recall was standing in front of my family's house in Everett, miles from the berry field. It was still afternoon, as though little or no time had actually passed, and I wasn't tired from walking.

Relieved, I walked up the steps to my front door and went inside. My mother was not home yet. My brother, sister, and father were not home, either. It was early afternoon, apparently.

I went inside and flopped upon my mother's bed on the first floor, since I did not feel well enough to walk up the steep stairs to my second-floor bedroom. I felt really out of it; racked with pain.

I waited until my mother came home and simply told her that I felt very sick to my stomach and that I'd come home early as a result. She gave me a lemon-lime soda, thinking it would settle my tummy.

When I felt even worse the next morning, she called our family physician, who told her to bring me to the hospital immediately for an appendectomy. At the hospital, our doctor called from his golf course to tell the staff to keep me on ice and prepped for emergency surgery while he finished the last nine holes.

By the time he arrived, my appendix had burst. Fortunately, I survived the experience and soon found myself recovering at home with ice cream, another of my mother's remedies for sick days.

I did not think much about my amazing trip from the berry field once I got home. I was just happy to be back to normal. I had a foggy memory of walking to Everett on railroad tracks that seemed to take me instantly to my home in the blink of an eye. I did not pay any attention to my lucky sense of direction and speedy trip. When you are twelve years old, you don't question finding your way home. You're only glad that you made it home safely. You don't try to analyze the details. In this case, I was unable to analyze the details.

That is, until the following summer. Then it hit me hard.

I was thirteen at the time and had been playing in the backyard of that same family house in Everett. I was practicing fly casting in the enclosed yard. I stopped to recline on my back in the plush grass and looked skyward into the summer sun. I suddenly remembered doing much the same thing on a similar summer afternoon one year earlier. Then I remembered walking on the railroad tracks.

Like a forgotten dream, little bits of the story started coming back to me. I remember that I had squinted at the sun during my walk on the rails and tried to determine what time of day it was and how long it might take me to get home before dark. I tried to remember more of this ordeal but found it difficult to do so.

I stood up and continued to practice fly casting. My neighbor, a retired butcher, had encouraged me to take up fly fishing. He had given me old copies of his fishing magazines and told me how to practice casting.

Standing in the back of the yard, I could cast all the way across the backyard to the white, wooden front fence, which was six feet tall and separated our backyard from the front yard. I watched the line zoom out as I did this. Sometimes it would reach the bottom of the fence and sometimes it would strike it. And then sometimes my line would fly all the way over the top of the fence.

When the fly on the end of my line caught the top of the wooden fence, I walked over to pry it loose and looked beyond the fence. On the other side of it, beyond the front yard, was the street that ran by our home. It was called Virginia Avenue, and there were other houses on either side of it.

That is when it really hit me. There were no train tracks in front of our house, and there never had been! At last, I remembered another part of the long-dismissed story about my journey home. I remember walking on train tracks with the idea that they would take me home.

I stood staring at the street in front of my house for some time, realizing that nothing about that entire trip from the berry field to my home made any sense to me. It was illogical. It was as though I had stepped outside of normal time and space. There was simply no other explanation for it.

The faint images of my strange encounter played in my mind as I continued to cast my fly rod again and again in the direction of Virginia Avenue. My elderly neighbor watched from a second-floor kitchen window next door and came out to comment on my progress. I believe I pretty much ignored him as I continued the casting motion over and over, my mind stuck on reliving the odd details that I'd suddenly recalled of my walk home the previous summer.

I had this strange idea that if I could go through the casting motions over and over that I would be able to define what had happened and reach some measure of inner satisfaction. I continued casting as I thought it through. But every cast was about the same, and the details of my walk on the railroad tracks to my front door never became apparent either. There would always be a hitch in these things, I decided.

So, I tried to tuck away the memories of my bizarre walk once again, for there were no railroad tracks in front of my home in Everett. It was an old mill town that had been created when a railroad man decided to build a track from his home in Saint Paul, Minnesota, to a settlement in the Pacific Northwest. Everett was part of the Washington Territory and featured the Snohomish River on one side and Port Gardner Bay on the other. One side of town subsequently became known as Riverside, while the other end of town become known as Bayside. I lived in the middle of this town, halfway between Riverside and Bayside.

The railroad tracks ran along the river in Riverside on one side of town and beside the bay in Bayside at the other end of town. The only place train tracks did not run in our town was down the middle of town—where I lived.

About three years later my family moved five miles north to the outskirts of Marysville, Washington. One of the first things I noticed about this new family home was that railroad tracks ran directly in front of the house, and you needed to drive over these tracks to get to our new home. Is this what I had been envisioning before I began my journey from the berry field years before? In any event, once again the memories of my bizarre journey home from the berry field four years earlier came flooding back to me.

I think this is how time works. It includes everything, including what we commonly consider our past, present, and future. It includes all outcomes and situations. It is not really fixed in the way we typically think it is. It is fluid and loops back on itself. Our perception allows us to fix our attention on only one instant as "now," but there are many other "now" instants on the loop.

I believe the little boy from the berry field somehow sidestepped into another parallel space and time—a space-time that he desperately needed and to which he somehow affixed his perception.

It's also possible, I suppose, that some guardian angel carried me home. Or maybe intelligent aliens abducted and transported me. But I do not remember anything like that. I do recall that I willed myself to be home and then suddenly I *was* home. In so doing I'd traveled miles from the berry field with no map to guide me, and at almost the same time that it had been when I'd left on my journey.

I do not think I could even find that berry field today. It was way out there in the country someplace.

There is quite a bit of synchronicity to this personal story.

Synchronicities seem to appear quite often in stories of time slips. The depth psychologist Carl Jung coined the term *synchronicity* to describe meaningful coincidences in our lives. Synchronicities tend to appear over and over, often in similar but slightly different situations, to bring our conscious attention to something of cosmic importance that we need to face. It seems that there is such a thing as happenstance, in Jung's evaluation, but at the same time he also sees significant meaning in our coincidences. They have karmic importance to our personal growth and understanding. It is apparently the way that the universe continues to bring matters of personal significance before our attention in repeated fashion until we get the message and deal with it.

Here's some more coincidence in my story of the train tracks from Saint Paul, Minnesota, to the Everett area in the state of Washington. I never thought I would leave the Pacific Northwest, but the company that employed me decided to move our office to the Twin Cities. The new office was in south Minneapolis.

I had been given scant notice that the owner of our company wanted to move us to the Twin Cities in Minnesota. A few months before he decided to make the move and informed us about it, I was on a business flight from the West Coast to New York. A flight attendant gave me a card and suggested that I call her for yoga training when I moved to the Twin Cities. She lived there and routinely flew from Portland to New York. I told her that I had no plans to be in the Twin Cities. She said to call her when I got there, however.

A few months later, my boss announced the move, and I indeed relocated to the Twin Cities. I called this flight attendant, to take her up on her offer of group and individual yoga classes. I had kept her card even though at the time I thought I'd never need it.

As another coincidence, this woman taught me yoga and how masters could learn to experience time and space outside of normal time and space. Her training was special and changed my life. In time, she moved away to start her own yoga school. I moved away, too, when I took a job in another state.

Four years later, however, I returned to Saint Paul. By coincidence, a business in my field offered me a job there; it was perfect for me. I took the job and moved into a Victorian house in the same neighborhood where railroad magnate James J. Hill had lived. In fact, the house was built during the same time that he'd been building his Great Northern Railroad from Saint Paul to Everett, Washington. He would have been right at home in the Victorian house. What a coincidence, right?

FOUR

Walking through Time Down Main Street

Some twenty years after my strange walk on the railroad tracks, I had put the story of my bizarre experience outside normal time and space pretty much out of mind. I had moved to Sandy, Oregon, where I worked as the young publisher of a community newspaper.

We found plenty of gritty stories about the people and place where we lived and worked, and thus we were a bit busy, without much time for introspection. Our little staff of five produced a weekly newspaper that fought for clean water, drug-free schools, and a proper visitor center for people interested in the pioneer heritage of our Barlow Trail pass over the mountain.

Looking back, we probably should not have taken ourselves so seriously, trying to expose shortcomings through the community paper. We might have taken more time to celebrate our neighbors and the beauty of our surroundings. But we were all young journalists and driven in our work. We had come through school about the time of Watergate and the Vietnam peace movement. So, we walked around town with serious expressions, always moving at a determined clip.

I found myself walking down Highway 26, the mountain pass that doubled as our main street, when the bottom fell out of my little place in that world. It was a clear, late spring afternoon with the sun burning down unusually hard. I was walking down this main street in

36

a business suit when everything around me suddenly changed.

Our main street was a long stretch of highway including about a mile or two of storefronts. It usually took me quite a while to walk the distance from one end to the other. I remember that I was walking west down to the end of the street, where our newspaper office sat behind a Chevrolet car dealership. The office was on a side road that led to the high school.

I did not complete the walk without major incident, however. Looking back now, I am amazed that I did not stumble or get struck by a car at any of the intersections. You see, I had stepped inadvertently into another time while I was walking down the sidewalk. Everything looked roughly the same in terms of general terrain, but the buildings looked older. The sidewalks were wooden. Suddenly I appeared to be in an earlier time.

Honestly, I do not know whether my physical body continued to move down the street when this happened or whether I actually disappeared from the street. If I did not disappear during my little time slip, then it probably would be safe to conclude that I was in two places and two times concurrently.

I have no witnesses to tell me that they saw a dazed young man walking down the street or narrowly missed bumping into him. I cannot image that I was terribly alert if I actually had managed to bilocate and continued to walk down the street during my time slip.

I can only tell you one thing for certain. When my consciousness shifted back to the here and now, I was surprised to see that I had walked the entire length of our main street. I found myself suddenly in front of our newspaper office, without any memory of having walked most of the way there.

Going into this time slip was a little like the situation twenty years earlier when I found myself walking on a railroad track and then suddenly was miles away. The distance I had traveled passed like the twinkling of an eye.

I don't know exactly where I went when I slipped outside normal space-time on that spring day, but I knew right away that my conscious awareness was somewhere other than the main street in Sandy, Oregon.

Just before it happened, my mind had become fairly clear. The sun baked down on my bare head. I seemed to disconnect from everything immediately around me, and I ceased to focus on the street and the moment. Walking became automatic. My mind became blank with no thoughts or impressions in it. I had no noticeable attachment to anything outside me or inside me. It was as though my consciousness had found a quiet, still place deep inside.

This was very much like the incident on the train tracks had been twenty years earlier. On that day, my fevered condition left me with a blankness inside me. When walking the tracks, I felt no attachment to the time, nor did I feel any attachment to the place. I walked like a robot without much consciousness. Thoughts inside me ceased. I had no sensory perception or inner thoughts to occupy my attention.

This state of mind, it seems to me in retrospect, seems germane to the time slips that I have personally experienced. If we hold together with our attention, as Carlos Castaneda wrote in *A Separate Reality,* then maybe the fragility of our present time and place is dependent on our conscious awareness of the details of our immediate surroundings. Maybe, as physicists have suggested, the chair we plainly see and consider solid in front of us supports our weight and maintains its physical form only with our concurrence that it's real and part of our reality, happening in what we experience in that instant as "now."

But maybe the physical world around us at the instant we experience as the present "now" in our life is not really that fixed and rigid. Maybe, as H. P. Blavatsky suggested in *The Secret Doctrine,* our physical world is plastic in the sense that it is not totally formed and inflexible. Maybe it is only half-formed and dependent on our conscious awareness, which is a key component in how flexible it is.

Most people can wrap their heads around the idea of the chair being actually in energetic motion and not all that solid in a physical sense. But the point here actually extends far beyond the chair and our belief that it will be solid enough to support us. The concept extends not only to space in the sense of materialism and matter in the physical sense but also the other side of space-time.

Time is also dependent on our conscious awareness. If we examine Albert Einstein's view of space-time, we see that he recognized the individual role of each person in perceiving time. He declared that the time interval between two events depends on the observer's frame of reference.

"Every reference-body," Einstein wrote in *The Theory of Relativity & Other Essays,* "has its own particular time; unless we are told the reference-body to which the statement of time refers, there is no meaning in a statement of the time of an event."

I would like to emphasize again that Einstein had read H. P. Blavatsky's book *The Secret Doctrine* and, as stated previously, reportedly wrote in its margins. Blavatsky spoke about the absolute reality from which we came, which is separate and apart from this material world. She spoke about the illusions of our physical world, that it's not what it appears to be. She suggested that the radiant light that initiates and sustains all of life infuses and enlivens manifest energy as much as pure unmanifest energy.

She didn't invent the concept of the half-formed material world, the plastic aspect of physical matter, but she did advance the notion. She based her writings on her understanding of *The Book of Dzyan,* a manuscript hidden in the Himalayas by ascetic masters and considered perhaps the oldest document on Earth. She had apparently seen the manuscript and subsequently received additional training in it by the ascetics who maintained it.

So, there could be many "now" instants; and they could all theoretically be happening simultaneously by our way of reckoning things. Where you focus your conscious attention is the "now" that you perceive. We are fixed, therefore, on the "now" that is before us in terms of our conscious awareness.

If we can suspend our perception and clear our consciousness to refocus on another instant, could we experience another "now" and another place? Do we truly hold the world together with our attention, as mystic author Carlos Castaneda suggested? Are there parallel realities we can visit if we shift our consciousness?

This is all something to think about, for sure.

I was thinking about nothing in particular when I stepped off a curb on my walk down Main Street that spring afternoon in Sandy, Oregon. My mind was totally clear and open.

When I put my foot down on that curb and entered an intersection at the far eastern end of town, I suddenly found myself in an altered state. I was no longer conscious of walking on that street nor of that spring afternoon. My whole vision of that space-time reality faded.

I wish I could tell you exactly where I found myself. I don't know where I went or what time period I had entered. I only knew that it was another time and place. I no longer had any sensation of being on the same street that I'd been on only a few moments before.

It must be said that we tend to think in terms of linear time as a rule, which probably is convenient in keeping things neat and orderly. It probably doesn't match the true nature of how Creation operates in the grand scheme of things, though. We like to measure everything to give ourselves a sense of comfort that we have things under control and that they are orderly. But what if space-time is not linear but instead filled with a lot of loops and turns? What if time curves back on itself? Most of us are probably not ready to step off the curb and into the uncertainty of a time and place that we have not measured.

But isn't that what exploration is all about—going beyond boundaries in search of discovery to increase our understanding? Early explorers of our physical world once feared that people could not travel too far for fear of falling off the edge of the world. They feared a treacherous land of dragons and other monsters that would endanger their survival in the land beyond. They thought that people could not go into space. They saw the world beyond their known world in linear terms. They could not envision anything more real than the ground on which they stood.

We are modern explorers who still press the barrier of known space. And now our understanding of space is interwoven with our understanding of reality as space-time. Our modern physicists suggest the likelihood of parallel universes and parallel realities very close to our own, just a breath away—as close as the other side of a tightly folded map.

Light strikes us here at this particular time and place, and we call this "now." But the light falls on the other side of this tightly folded map, initializing and actualizing other instances of space-time. Others will realize *that* as their own version of "now." What if we cross this fold in the space-time continuum?

That's probably what I did on that late spring afternoon on Mount Hood in Oregon. The sensation was like crossing into another time and space where nothing I had previously experienced on the main street in town applied or held any meaning for me.

Again, I cannot describe where I was during my departure or the relative time period that I occupied briefly during my absence. I know that I was momentarily living a life in another place and living a slightly different life. That life and that place seemed every bit as real as my life as a community journalist in Sandy, Oregon. Maybe it was the same town but another time? I know that it looked different. There were no sidewalks, only dirt roads with boardwalks in front of the stores. The buildings were different, too. They were wooden structures, not as modern. I saw no people there. The sky looked the same. The mountain looked the same. I do not think I was anywhere distant. It was quiet there, uncluttered, peaceful, and pleasant. I heard no sounds.

In a way, however, it was unsettling. I was disoriented. I felt that I did not belong there, yet I was comfortable to just be there.

I soaked it all in, trying to orient myself. I wondered at one point if I was dreaming. Then I remembered that I had been walking and had been quite awake on the sidewalk in Sandy moments earlier. I tried to look around and make some sense of things. I wondered what had happened to me on that Oregon sidewalk that I should suddenly find myself in this other place. Suddenly I worried about the man, the other me, who had been walking on the sidewalk moments earlier. Was he all right? I wondered whether I was that same man or experiencing life as another man.

This sudden concern about my condition and how I had left my place on the sidewalk somehow snapped me back into my body on the main street of Sandy. I thought it would be where I'd left it at the east end of town, when I'd begun my walk. I assumed initially that I had walked body and soul into another place and would return to the same spot from which I'd departed.

I was surprised to realize that I had walked all the way across town while my consciousness was somewhere else. This made no sense to me at all. How could I have negotiated traffic and crossed intersections on the continuation of my walk down the main street?

Honestly, I do not know to this day how long I experienced this other time and place on that day. The easy answer would be to say that it took as long as it takes a man walking normally down Main Street to travel the several blocks from east to west. But I wasn't walking normally. And I wasn't aware of the moment when I started to drift somewhere else, so I had no way to judge how much ordinary time had elapsed during my strange departure.

I just know that I had finished lunch at the east end of town just before starting my walk back to our newspaper office and found it almost the end of the workday when I reached the office. That would suggest that I was gone for more than a couple of hours.

I cannot account for the time I was gone.

That is what makes this odd tale sound like a slip in time. When most people experience time shifts, they often say that they cannot account for time in the day when they weren't present. They cannot account for where they were, only that it seemed to be somewhere outside their normal time and place. It was like they popped out and then popped back in.

And that is what it was like for me. Maybe I bilocated. Maybe I was dream walking. How can I ever really know?

I just know that when I got to the end of the sidewalk and turned up the side road to reach our newspaper office, I did a little double take. A shiver went down my spine. I thought about how this place had looked in the past and how it would look in the future.

Years later I visited Sandy to see if it was pretty much as I remembered it. Many things looked the same. The main street was still a long sidewalk with businesses on both sides. But the Chevrolet car dealership that had blocked the view of our newspaper office from the main street was gone. The newspaper was no longer located in the building behind that lot either. The car lot and newspaper occupied that spot only for a specific and relatively short period in the time continuum—during the relatively short time span that I worked in that town.

For many weeks and months after my strange experience on the sidewalk in Sandy, I worried about my condition and whether I was healthy and normal. Had I hallucinated? Had I walked in my sleep? Had I lost my mind? Had I walked out of my body or abandoned my body, permitting my consciousness to idly wander? If so, this seemed reckless and irresponsible.

I began to wonder whether I should be tested medically. Was there something wrong with me? It is a little disconcerting to lose control of yourself like that. People like the comfort of maintaining control over themselves and their environment. We like to be able to account for our every movement and every moment of our day. We like to measure things out, staying safely inside our little three-dimensional boxes.

Maybe that is why we lock ourselves in our houses at night.

FIVE

In a Dark Room

I tried to put my crazy adventure down Main Street out of mind when I returned to work at the newspaper building. For some time, I continued to wonder whether I should be professionally "checked over" by medical people or psychologists to determine whether I was okay. I really did not want to believe that I had experienced some sort of breakdown and might do so again. But without any damage or loss from the incident, it was simply easier to let it go and forget about the whole thing.

Perhaps it was some aberration or anomaly that could not be resolved or interpreted within a normal frame of reference. It did not fit the norm or provide me with anything that I could discuss with other people without drawing odd stares, so I just dropped it.

Besides, there were plenty of other things to keep me busy on a community newspaper. Unlike daily newspapers or broadcast media, community newspapers traditionally work without syndication services or feature services to augment local coverage. Typically, a small newspaper staff on a small budget works long hours to cover all the local news in a serious and respectful manner. Our little staff in Sandy included some wonderful people when I was there, including a future daily newspaper editor who later became the information director for a major university. While in Sandy, we all worked from morning until late at night and rarely with any time off.

Part of what we did there at our little newspaper office was to develop and print photographs for use in the published articles. We remodeled the building to accommodate a darkroom, and in it everyone developed and printed their own pictures. I was no exception. In fact, I had outfitted the darkroom with some of my own equipment, which I ultimately donated to the newspaper when I left Oregon.

Often, I would develop my film at the end of a long day and hang my negatives to dry before processing them in an enlarger. This was in the old days of black-and-white photojournalism.

One night, some months after my incident on the sidewalk, I found myself processing film in the darkroom. I was all alone in the building. Some of our staff was probably still working at that hour, covering night meetings or meeting with people they couldn't reach during normal business hours. But our building was quiet as I worked silently in the darkroom that night.

Usually, such darkroom work would occur quickly and without incident. We knew when we processed our film which pictures were worth developing. We did not need to examine a proof sheet. We'd just hang the developed rolls of film to dry, suspended from a wire by heavy clips. Following that, we'd look carefully at the best negatives and then print a decent photo from them in the photo enlarger. The enlargement process transferred a negative image onto receiving paper for a positive print. In our case, we would print through a vacuum easel screen to make a print with dots. Ink would darken the dots to form a patterned print. The dot pattern in our black-and-white newspaper press runs is like the dot pattern in your television screen if you look closely at the internal patterns.

Since this darkroom process had become routine and simple, we could work in the darkroom without much thought. We would sort of put our minds on autopilot in the dark there. We became proficient at working without light. In our darkroom, we had just one little red light that would not affect the film processing. The exposed film had to be loaded into a developing tank in total darkness without even the red light. We got to where we could move around the room without seeing well, because we knew where everything was. That included a wooden stool where I would sit when I developed the negatives. Once the negatives were loaded in darkness, I would continue to sit with the lights out.

I would sit on that wooden stool after loading the roll of film onto a metal spool and fitting it into a sealed metal can that I filled with developer. Then I would squint in the dim light provided by that single red lamp to set the timer. When time had expired, the process required us to dump the developing chemicals and then rinse the can before putting fixer in it.

Sitting on that stool for a few minutes with the can in my hand, all I really had to do was gently agitate it periodically and wait for the timer to alert me as to when to switch to the rinse phase. Naturally, it was important not to underdevelop or overdevelop the film; however, there was little chance of this happening because the timer always proved loud enough to alert me when the time between cycles had expired.

None of that process transpired in a timely manner on this particular night, however. All I really remember is loading the can with the film and developer, setting the timer, and then sitting on that wooden stool.

I don't know how long I sat there, but when I returned to normal consciousness, I realized that the timer had been buzzing for some time. I felt that I had been somewhere very distant for a while. I naturally worried how long the buzzer had tried to gain my attention. I had no way in that darkroom to tell just how overdeveloped the film might be, so I quickly rinsed the metal container and then put fixer into the can. I figured my roll of film might be ruined.

Once the film had run through the fixer and then had been set under running water for a final rinse, I ran out of the darkroom to check the big clock on the wall. I had been sitting on that stool half an hour beyond the recommended time, completely out of it! I don't know exactly where I was for all of that missing time, but my consciousness had been somewhere else.

I know that I hadn't been sleeping, however, because I held the film can safely. I probably even agitated it periodically while I sat on that stool. But my consciousness was clearly somewhere else, as it had been on that prior occasion when I'd taken that walk down Main Street.

I lay down in the outer room while the film went through its final rinse. It was very overdeveloped, and it would later prove to be difficult to print anything recognizable from it.

I reclined on my back outside the darkroom and tried to get into a mental space where I could collect my thoughts as to where my consciousness might have gone. I did not want the incident to remain a mystery like my bizarre incident in Sandy had been.

My quiet reflection after this darkroom experience did bring it into focus somewhat. I had always been conscious of sitting on that stool in the quietness of that darkroom. But in the minutes that I seemed to lose my consciousness and go somewhere else, I felt that I was in a room that was more vacant than the darkroom. It was a larger room with no photo equipment, no timers, no red safe light, no counters for working, and no sink. It was a bare room with four walls. I was vaguely aware of being in this quiet, deserted room for several minutes without anything happening.

This might seem odd, but I would add that many people who experience missing minutes in the middle of their day have similarly vague recollections. People who report being abducted by extraterrestrials often have great difficulty recalling where they have been and what they encountered in the moments they were gone.

They find it difficult to account for the missing gaps in the normal linear timeline. This time is time interrupted. I suspect that the experience seems so unusual and hard to accept that they feel unable to properly process the information and analyze it. We tend to analyze things in our mundane world with our physical brain, not our heightened consciousness. (I would suggest that our physical brain is often unable to deal with what it encounters.)

I don't believe I was abducted by aliens or that I was daydreaming. I might have been bilocating, but I was fully erect on the stool all during the event and continued holding the film can. I do not really know whether I continued to agitate the film canister by shaking it periodically during the minutes in question.

After I was able to print some very dense photos from the overdeveloped film, I continued to ponder these two incidents (my walk down the main street and my time in the darkroom), which apparently were time slips. All I knew was that I could not adequately account for the lost time that had occurred on these two occasions.

I decided that I could not continue to lose time in this fashion and risk appearing out of sorts to others. Most people expect things to happen in a timely fashion, it seems. Why else would we measure it so carefully and hold people accountable for their time? I now realize how silly this standard of measurement is, because time as we normally conceive of it is very arbitrary. The time that elapses while I'm listening to music or boating on a river doesn't necessarily reflect a standard measure of time. Einstein tried to explain the relativity of time in very human ways. For instance, the time a man might spend with someone as exciting as Marilyn Monroe wouldn't be perceived in the same way that time spent in a dentist's chair might be perceived, or in trying to put out a fire. In the former case with Marilyn Monroe, time might probably fly by, and in the latter two instances, a few minutes might feel like an hour. Time seems to pass slowly or quickly depending on our personal feelings about the situation in which we find ourselves and our perception of it.

In the grander scheme of things, glaciers take as long as they take to form and melt. Rocks erode very slowly at their own pace. Things take just as long as they need to in order to change and transform. It's the same with *our* transformation, I suppose. It will happen in its own good time. You can't clock on a stopwatch how long things might be required to happen.

But we like to measure everything. I was like that, too, as a young journalist fighting deadlines every day. I also did not like the apparent loss of control that these experiences engendered, as I found myself again and again unable to account not only for my time but also for my presence. Most people like to feel that they are engaged and involved. I felt that I was losing control.

So, I panicked and decided to turn myself over to medical professionals so they could poke and probe me for some possible problem. I wondered whether I should turn to a psychologist or medical people at the hospital. The one thing I didn't want to do was relate my two recent incidents to anyone who could tie me into a bed or a straitjacket.

Mind you, I didn't mention my strange encounters to anyone on our newspaper staff, either. I figured there was no telling what a curious journalist might do with stories of this sort. Nor did I mention the matter to anyone in my community, friends, or family. I didn't want anyone to hear about any of it until I could get some sort of handle on it myself. And I was beginning to worry that the answers would not be easy.

Now that I am many years down the road from my days on Mount Hood, I can see that no matter what, some answers do not come that easily. It has taken me a long time to try to make sense of my little time slip in Sandy.

At the time these incidents happened, I gave myself a couple of days to sort things out. I figured that I could check myself into the community hospital in Gresham, Oregon, over the weekend and go through a battery of tests to see what might be wrong with me.

I asked my personal physician in Sandy if tests in the hospital were a good idea. I did not provide any details of my encounters but simply said that I appeared to blank out now and then and wanted to see if everything was medically okay.

My doctor was an elderly country doctor in his late seventies. People loved him, which made it hard for him to retire. He never made appointments but asked anyone who wanted his attention to show up in his waiting room at 9:00 a.m. He would then put all his office chairs in a circle and work his way around the circle, evaluating everyone eventually but prioritizing those who needed urgent attention. I guess this was his approach to triage.

The individual to be treated would then be brought into his treatment room, where he typically would spend about ten minutes on that person and then charge them ten dollars. If you insisted that you should receive some prescription medicine, he would hand you a few medical samples from his office, which usually were enough free pills to last you no more than three days.

He was a no-nonsense country doctor who thought that less medical treatment was best.

When I got into his morning circle and worked my way inside for treatment, he told me that he would set up my visit to the Gresham hospital. He would not accompany me there, however. In fact, he said it was generally a good idea to avoid hospitals altogether, if a person could. He added that it was a good idea to avoid medical doctors, too, whenever possible. He said doctors often did too much, or they did more harm than good. Hospitals, he said, were a dangerous place to go, because people could come out sicker than when they went in.

Anyway, that is what he told me. Foolishly, I checked into the hospital that weekend anyway. What did I have to lose?

Fortunately, my country doctor back in Sandy had explained my concerns to them, as well as what I wanted done. Thus, I didn't need to justify why I was checking into the hospital for extensive exploratory tests. I did, however, need to confirm to them that I could pay for all of the costly tests, whatever the cost, given that my excellent medical insurance, provided to me via my job at the newspaper, paid for everything.

Given that I had asked the hospital for a complete workup with every test they could throw at me over two days, I kept busy once I'd checked in. The hardest part initially was figuring how to wear that silly gown that only ties in the back. I remember some very pleasant nurses who immediately put me to bed and told me to relax until someone came to get me for a test. I didn't need to wait long. The tests kept me busy for two solid days. I was the one to call it quits after the second day, because they could always think of another test in another lab at the hospital. I needed to get back to our newspaper.

Each morning I was brought pills with which to start the day, pills later in the day, and pills to help me sleep at night. Honestly, I could not see much purpose in any of those pills. As it was, I would already start each day bright and alert and continued to feel strong and healthy throughout the day. I had no trouble sleeping at night.

Consequently, I stashed every one of these unnecessary pills in the little bedside table next to the tissues that I never used but which would be added to my bill anyway. After the second day, I was approached by a male doctor and the nurse who had been assigned to my room. The doctor complained that I had not taken any of my medication. I assumed someone on staff had gone through my bedside drawer or caught me hiding the pills there.

I asked about the purpose of the medication. The doctor responded with words to the effect that medical professionals had prescribed those pills and that I should take them without question.

When I quipped that I didn't need pills to wake up in the morning, pills to get me through the day, and pills to make me sleep, the doctor only frowned. This was my only contact with a medical doctor in my two-day stay, so I thought I would make the most of our little visit.

I asked him if he would feel good about taking the medication that had been given to me. When he answered in the affirmative, I scooped the pills out of the drawer and handed them to him.

"Knock yourself out," I said. "They're all yours, then."

He frowned again.

I asked what they had determined about my condition after my tests. The doctor said the tests were inconclusive but that they could run more tests.

I told him that I was finished with tests and wanted to leave the hospital. As I recall, I left rather abruptly. That saved them a few sleeping pills, at least.

My little account of exploratory tests in a medical hospital is not intended to criticize hospital practice or protocol. They all followed established hospital medical protocol, I suppose. My point is that you cannot explain with medical tests something as personal and metaphysical as time shifts.

SIX

A Brother
and Sister Reunion

My mother told me the most amazing personal story of time travel; it involved her and her brother. It was a vision that she could not get out of her head, so she told me the story year after year. Even now it does not seem to make much sense to me. It did not make much sense to her, either, even after years of reflection. But that is the way things appear to us out of time and space: like an upside-down world where we have no solid bearings to help us make sense of the things we see.

To understand the closeness of my mother and her older brother, I need to tell you a little about their family and the farm where they spent their childhood. It was a wheat farm in North Dakota, a rural area settled by German and Norwegian immigrants for the most part. My mother and uncle were third-generation Prussians on their father's side and third-generation Norwegians on their mother's side. The farm was their security in the new land.

My mother and her brothers grew up playing together because the nearest neighbors lived very far away. They either walked or cross-country skied to school, which was located a few miles away. When it snowed hard in the winter, they could not see out the windows. With the snow piled so high, they had to walk from the house to the barn and other shelters by clutching a clothesline strung between the buildings.

The little community church was where everyone came together.

Children were born at home, usually with no record of birth except an entry in a book at the little white church.

Because there were so many children in their family, as with many farm families, they watched after each other while the men were working the fields and the women were cooking, canning, and cleaning. My mother had two older brothers, and two young brothers whom she took under her wing like a mother hen. When they got older, my mother and her older brother would attend high school away from home, boarding with a family in a neighboring town.

It was a safe and secure environment in many ways. During the years of the Great Depression they always had a garden, due to their mother's green thumb, and they always had animals for milk and meat. Hobos would hop off the train to eat a sandwich at their back porch. For many people in that time and place, life was not easy.

My mother left the family farm after high school during the war years to work at a Catholic hospital in Duluth, Minnesota. One of her older brothers, Vernon, had already left home to join the Navy as a medic stationed in the Philippines.

One day shortly after Vern had shipped out, my mother had what she called a strange vision. The way she remembered the incident, she was standing just outside the family's house. She started to walk toward the barn and then looked up when something rather strange caught her attention. She said the whole scene seemed a little out of sorts, almost surreal. Things around her did not appear quite as they had a moment prior. It seemed like a different time of the day and another season.

Out of nowhere, she said, she saw a young man walking to the gate of the corral.

He was older than she was but not yet middle-aged. She noticed that he was wearing a white short-sleeve shirt. He looked athletic and trim. Strangely, the man looked familiar to her, although she could not place him. Because he was some distance from her with his face turned down to open the gate, she was not able to see him clearly.

Then the gate swung open, and the man disappeared. She blinked her eyes in disbelief. He had seemed to simply vanish right in front of her, and she could not reconcile what she had seen. She ran back into the house to find someone to tell but found herself alone.

When she went back outside, she found the gate to the corral shut and nobody in sight. Also, the scene had reverted to the sort of day and season she had initially observed before the man made his strange appearance. She ran toward the corral area to try to find the mysterious man or some clue about what she had witnessed. Curiously, she found nothing out of sorts. Once again, she found herself completely alone and without any explanation.

After that, she convinced herself that it had been a sort of daydream. She decided that there had never been any young man in a white shirt walking through the gate. It was some sort of mirage. Maybe the light had played tricks on her, she thought. Maybe it was the summer heat affecting her. Clearly, there had been nobody there.

However, the incident was printed indelibly on her mind. She knew what she had seen and could not forget it. The memory and uncertainty of what she had witnessed would remain on her mind for many years.

When she tried to sort things out immediately after the incident, she did what people often do when trying to reconcile things they witness that don't seem to add up. She went over the vision again and again, searching for clues to piece together the puzzle.

My mother's first reaction on the day of the incident was to find someone to help her make sense of what had just happened. When she did get a chance to talk to someone about it later in the day, she merely hinted at something she *might* have seen out of the corner of one eye. She pestered family members later in the day to see if they might have seen a young man in a white shirt on the premises. She asked other family members who such a person might have been. Nobody could help her, however.

So she just dropped the subject, out of fear of looking odd and unbalanced. She tucked away the memory, trying to forget it. Still, she knew what she had witnessed. It was very clear to her, and she couldn't shake it. The image had been very vivid and very real to her, if only for a moment. It played on her subconscious mind, causing her to have recurring dreams about it for many years. The more she had this recurring dream, the more she questioned whether the whole memory of seeing the young man in the white shirt that day had been nothing more than a dream in the first place.

When she completed her high school years in the neighboring town, she left North Dakota and the family farm to work beside the north shore of Lake Superior in Minnesota. The hospital where she worked offered her a grand view of the great lake from the third-floor obstetrics ward, which was her post. She would look out that window into the vast depth of the lake for hours, wondering where her life would take her and wondering whether she would ever see her brothers again.

Again, the war years were a difficult time for many people, including civilians back home. Everyone must have felt rudderless back then. My mother left her job at the Duluth hospital, which overlooked the lake and followed her aunt to Everett, Washington. Several relatives had found jobs there. When they both lived on the family farm, her aunt had helped my mother prepare a daily spread of food for the fieldworkers during harvest. Her aunt took my mother into her new home in Everett, and my mother lived there with her aunt and cousins before meeting a returning soldier. She moved out when she married my father, who was home from the war. So many returning soldiers were starting over, and my mother wondered when she would see any of her brothers again.

In the meantime, her two older brothers had grown into men. The elder one was taking an active role in running the family farm, having taken over this responsibility due to their father's failing health. Vernon, her other older brother and in the navy, had served as a navy medic in the Philippines, where he found jungle conditions after Japanese occupation very difficult. Many men stationed in the jungle were in poor health. Whatever toll deprivation and oppression placed on them was made worse by jungle diseases.

Vern was lucky to make it out of the Philippines in one piece and happy to take off his uniform at the end of the war. He'd made many friends in the navy, and they decided to travel across the country at the end of the war to celebrate their new freedom. A lot of men seemed to do that following their service. They would take some time to collect themselves after the ordeal with a sort of victory tour through the countryside.

Vern and his friends found their way to his sister's home in Everett, Washington. There Vern met his brother-in-law and two young nephews for the first time. He was happy, carefree, and seemingly healthy.

Unfortunately, Vern did not realize that he had developed tuberculosis in the Philippines. The former medic would whoop it up in town part of the day with his two navy buddies and then return to the little house in Everett to spend time with his sister and her family. It was a small house, but his sister found places for all three navy veterans to sleep for several nights.

Vern seemed delighted to spend time with his sister's two toddlers and played with them every chance he got, sharing his contagious laugh and sense of fun with the two boys. The younger of the two— my younger brother—had a severe breathing problem, which was a family concern. Consequently, Vern had to be careful not to overtax the toddler in all the fun and play.

When Vern and his comrades left, my younger brother took a turn for the worse, finding it even harder to breath. The family soon learned that his condition was now complicated by tuberculosis. Vern would soon discover that he himself suffered from tuberculosis as well.

He was otherwise in good health, young, and fit. He'd apparently lived with tuberculosis for some time. Consequently, it didn't derail him as quickly as it did my younger brother, who died at the age of two. The local hospital advised my parents to rush my gasping brother to the university hospital in Seattle, where they had a better respirator that was more suitable for a child. Driving at breakneck speed down the old highway with a police escort one night, they still arrived at the Seattle hospital too late.

The funeral for my younger brother Darrell James was preceded by the funeral for Uncle Vernon back in North Dakota. I remember traveling with my mother and father to the family farm for the ceremony and the family gathering afterward. We stayed a few days.

This was my mother's only visit to the family farm in many years. While only five years old myself, I remember the visit very well. I recall taking a bath in a horse trough, which relatives there found hilarious. I remember the comfortable old farmhouse and its porch. I remember Grandmother's huge garden. And I remember the chicken coop, the barn, and the corral.

My mother stared out from the house porch at the corral one hot summer afternoon and fixed her gaze on its gate. She seemed almost transfixed, as though deep in thought. She was remembering that other summer afternoon years ago when she'd stood by the house and seen what looked like a young man in a white short-sleeve shirt open the gate. She said nothing about her reflection; but when we returned home, she began to tell me about her strange vision again. Maybe talking about such an odd occurrence with your little boy was not as threatening as discussing it seriously with another adult.

She said she had experienced a sort of flashback to her earlier vision at the family farm, and with this the pieces of the puzzle began to fall into place. She realized that the man in the white shirt had been her brother Vernon. It was not the young Vernon she remembered when they were youngsters together back on the farm but a young man fresh from the navy, trim and vibrant. She knew that man now. She had not been able to recognize him years earlier because he had been just a boy back then.

My mother never spoke of her strange vision, as she called it, as a moment out of time. I don't believe anyone she knew ever used that term or considered the possibility of time shifts either. Instead, they talked about visions, strange images, imagination, and dreams. They had no other frame of reference.

It does make sense, however, that her brother would want to finally return home for the family reunion on the occasion of his physical passing. And it would seem logical for him, upon his return to his boyhood home, to open the gate and walk through it once and for all. And it's only logical that he would shut the gate after passing through it. He had disappeared and wasn't coming back.

My mother continued to discuss this story with me for many years, so I know it had left a lasting impression on her. She felt that it was meant only for her to experience.

A dear friend and colleague of mine, Frank Joseph, has written many fine books on synchronicity as meaningful coincidence. The phenomenon of synchronicity seems to have karmic significance for the person who experiences it, in his view. We might think of it as the cosmos giving us repeated clues about things that we need to contemplate in our lives so as to grow in depth and understanding. Maybe that was the case here. Certainly, there seems to be a certain amount of synchronicity in my mother's story if we consider the repeating pattern of events and circumstances involved.

Historically, people would often shun, ignore, or doubt the divine insight and direction offered to them by ancient oracles. They would choose to direct their own lives and find their own way along life's path. We see in classical Greek mythology how people would sometimes need to see things of personal importance dramatically revealed to them. For instance, the wrong decision by Paris when asked by Zeus to name which of the goddesses was the most beautiful forced him into the Trojan War. He chose Aphrodite, who promised him the earthly beauty Helen of Troy in exchange for deciding in her favor. His answer infuriated the other goddesses and his capture of Helen launched the war. A similar bad choice during the Trojan War was made by King Odysseus. His arrogance and defiance of the gods caused his ship home to become drastically off-course in storms sent his way by the god of the sea. This long journey home forced him to confront many challenges to finally bring him to his senses.

Similarly, the ancient Hindu story in the Bhagavad Gita shows a warrior who is personally shown the impact of his choices by the lord, who acts as his chariot driver through several battles. It seems that the cosmic solution to getting people to confront the choices of their lives is to repeatedly put them in a position that makes them focus on the issues associated with those choices. For many of us, these obstacles might seem like the craziest kind of bad luck and timing, but these myths imply that they are rather an opportunity put in our path to force us to focus and make good choices.

My mother was no warrior, world explorer, or Trojan princess. She was, however, a woman who clearly saw some significance in a strange situation that had been placed in front of her one warm summer day. Even in her declining senior years when she was put into a nursing home and could remember little more than her own name, she remembered the man who mysteriously appeared in a white shirt at the gate and then disappeared.

I recall visiting her in the nursing home to sit with her and take her for wheelchair rides through the North Dakota town where she lived her final days. Outwardly, she appeared largely unresponsive to people and things around her while other residents of the nursing home watched television or looked at the fish tank.

An attendant would try to engage her in conversation or would toss her a huge lightweight beach ball when she sat on the sofa. She would just stare ahead of her as though lost in thought. She would continue to do this until the attendants would take her into the dining room to eat or to her room to sleep.

On one of her final days, I wheeled her to a nearby restaurant for a nice Sunday dinner. She ate and smiled but otherwise spoke very little. Then she leaned over the rail of her wheelchair to speak. "You seem like a nice man," she told me. "Are you my brother?"

Her brother Vern was always on her mind, it seemed, even at the end when so little memories remained. It was as though she always expected him to suddenly pop into her life again as a young man.

This story reminds me of an old calculator I once found in an abandoned bank building that I converted to a newspaper office in Petersburg, Alaska. I plugged the adding machine into the wall and gave it a problem to solve. It continued to grind away for hours, unable to find the answer. I thought about unplugging it but instead just let it continue trying to work through the problem. I was concerned that it was stuck in that one spot and that it would only keep returning to it if I didn't let it reach some conclusion. It never came up with an answer but started to smoke. Before I recognized it and pulled the plug, the room was filled with smoke. The smoke-filled building was reported, and the island's volunteer fire department responded immediately.

I think that old bank calculator was a little like my mother's mind grinding away at a problem she could not easily solve. But she just kept trying.

At one point, like my mother, I was tempted to classify her story of the strange vision in a way that seemed more familiar to me. I referred to it for some time as a ghostly presence. Ghosts usually haunt a specific time and do not travel back in time from what I have heard of such sightings. But I imagine that nonphysical spirits would not be restricted by our normal laws of physics and could move freely.

No, I think it's more likely that my mother as a girl saw her brother in another time when she took one step off her farmhouse porch and suddenly saw everything in front of her with a slightly different hue. The time of day and season seemed a little different to her just as the strange man appeared and opened the gate. The vision ended when he disappeared in front of her eyes.

I submit that she likely experienced a time shift.

SEVEN

Time Shifts Experienced by Writer/Explorer Frank Joseph

Frank Joseph, from the Upper Mississippi Valley, is a writer and explorer of Earth mysteries who has experienced many apparent slips in time during his extensive travels around the world. I have known Frank for many years as a trained journalist who has written more than thirty books, and I trust the personal observations of this man. Strangely, there seems to be an apparent pattern to his time shifts that might offer clues about what conditions produce them.

His first experience happened in Chicago when he was twenty-seven years old. He was standing at the corner of 67th Street in southwest Chicago. It was a busy intersection of small businesses, gas stations, apartment complexes, and the spacious grounds of Holy Cross Hospital. It was a bright, crisp, late autumn afternoon, near sundown, in 1972, a day that Frank remembers vividly even now.

He remembers relaxing and clearing his mind as his gaze wandered across California Avenue to Marquette Park, a public park of benches, pavilions, trees, and historical monuments. He had walked its winding footpaths countless times before.

On this day, however, he was overcome by a calm serenity, mindlessly admiring the park's loveliness. Suddenly, the relentless sounds of the city became muted, and the blight of endless city vehicles faded before his gaze. Even Marquette Park itself seemed to lose all of its posted signs, bike paths, benches, and stone memorials. It was suddenly replaced by thick, primeval forests and, in spots, the last rays of the setting sun streaked through dense trees.

"A perfect, almost frightening silence totally pervaded the changed scene," Frank recalls. "There was not a single bird song or rustle of wind, as though a cosmic-sized dome of glass had been lowered over Chicago."

Frank reflects that what he saw was probably the way the park once looked long before people arrived there. "It was as though a filmy veil had been briefly tossed over my head," Frank recalls, "draping over my eyes, radically changing the world (or at least this small part of it). Then almost as quickly, it was whisked off, completely taking away with it the brief vision."

Just as suddenly the scene shifted back to city streets, traffic, buildings, and a modern park in the twentieth century. "It left me stunned and questioning my mental health," Frank remembers. "But the potent reality of the moment could not be dismissed then or now. It seems to have been less of a psychotic episode than a rift in time occasioned at least partially by my untypical state of peaceful mind, brought on by the attractive interplay of light and trees."

In his heart, Frank said, it felt like a thank you gift from the unknown, from a loving consciousness or what the ancient Romans called *genius loci,* "the spirit of place"—the spectral custodian of sacred sites. "I felt then," he recalls, "blessed by the experience, which continues to personally affirm the reality of such things."

Time Slip, Japan, 1996

Some twenty-four years later the same man experienced a similar event on the opposite side of the world. During Frank Joseph's first trip to Japan, he climbed to the top of Atago Hill, the highest vantage point in Tokyo. What he saw was just as unforgettable and surreal as his Chicago park experience had been years earlier.

"I had not come for the panorama of the capital," Frank recalls, "but because previous research indicated Atago was associated in myth with the country's earliest settlers. In their story of arriving after a natural catastrophe at sea, suggestions of lost Atlantis were implied by the very name of the hill itself.

"I was surprised and a bit freaked," Frank relates, "to see that the entire summit was one large cemetery, although nothing suggested deep antiquity except a very old, dark, mysterious Shinto shrine far below at the base of the hill. But the building was closed, preventing any investigation. At the top of Atago, views of Tokyo sprawling out in all its urban chaos were spectacular.

"I was about to begin my descent after lingering there only a few minutes, when that unseen veil once more floated on my head and over my eyes," Frank recalls, hearkening back to his earlier experience at the Chicago park. "The immense city with its rising traffic noise suddenly vanished and was replaced by a thick, dark green forest extending in every direction to the horizon in perfect silence. Then it quickly faded away, returning to modern Tokyo in all its overcrowded modernity, as the veil-like sensation passed."

A Familiar Landscape, Greece, 1991

Frank Joseph has traveled the world to explore ancient mysteries for his many books. Along the way, he has personally experienced several time shifts similar to his sidesteps into a veiled, silent past in Chicago and Tokyo.

In the early nineties, Frank took a ferryboat from the Greek mainland to the small island of Delos, which he was visiting to research ancient Atlantis. From the early Bronze Age some five thousand years ago, Delos was known as the navel of the world. It was where the pre-Hellenic flood hero, Deucalion, supposedly landed after surviving the Great Deluge.

Delos subsequently became the crown jewel of the Aegean Sea, a location of great wealth, artistic greatness, and religious power until the fall of classical civilization in the middle of the fifth century. The island has since become an antiquarian paradise of preserved ruins.

As Frank stepped off the ferry at Delos, he felt a wave of both shock and sadness sweep across him. "I almost uttered aloud in horror, 'Everything's wrecked!'" Frank recalls. Then he rationalized his first impression with the realization that he was visiting what amounted to an archaeological site, not some amusement park.

"As I strolled among the fallen columns and broken statuary," Frank remembers, "I could not discard an emotion of aghast despair, as though I was returning home and finding my neighborhood totally destroyed. Feelings of intimate, inexplicable identification gripped me."

He had planned to stay only a single afternoon, but he stayed the next four days, wandering like a ghost among the ruins. He said he was looking for something he couldn't identify, as though trying to remember something apparent but long forgotten.

Still, he could not shed that deep sense of tragic loss. "While neither my eyes nor ears perceived anything out the ordinary," Frank recalls, "my heart resonated with those other times that my conscious mind found too unclear to grasp."

Return to Ancient Troy, 1991

In 1991, Frank visited the town of Çanakkale on the northern Mediterranean coast of Turkey. It was there that the ruins of a late Bronze Age site associated with the ancient city of Troy were found buried within the ancient city of Hissarlik.

The location today is a public archaeological zone, and only a small fraction of the entire Trojan capital has been excavated from it. Little remains of an urban center that was badly burned by invaders and later looted and reoccupied with new construction.

Despite these losses, the location still reveals part of the ancient city's iconic sloping walls in addition to graceful columns, a small theater from the Roman era, and early foundations. The city stood then, as it does today, atop a high hill that overlooks the sea that carried a vast Greek attack fleet some thirty-two centuries earlier.

Frank Joseph's travels brought him there at a perfect time in a sense. With few curators around to restrict his movements, Frank was able to freely explore broken remnants of the doomed city on his own. The ancient site was deserted as far as he could tell.

"I sat on the edge of a stone rampart that faced the Aegean Sea and the beach far below," Frank recalls. He sat there, reading about the sea invasion in a copy of the *Iliad* he'd brought along. "I was gradually distracted by an unusual, distant sound."

Initially he paid little attention to the faint interruption until he realized it was the music of a flute, like the sound that a shepherd's pipe would make. "I stood up to scan the beach and adjacent farmland," Frank said, "but I saw no one in any direction. The wispy, melancholy tune continued for another two or three minutes, then gradually vanished on the wind." Oddly, as Frank recalls, nobody was working in the adjacent farmlands, strolling the beach, or visiting the Trojan ruins. He seemed to be quite alone, which made the mysterious sound of the flute hard to explain.

He returned the next day in hopes of hearing more strange music, but never heard the flute again.

"Such things are beyond proving to others," Frank admits. "Who can appreciate such an event unless they have had a similar experience?"

Frank today concludes that his clairaudience indicated that he had experienced a rift in time.

Mysterious Encounter, Rock Lake, Wisconsin, 1995

Clairaudience is the perception of sound beyond the range of conventional human hearing. This general definition includes a diversity of audio phenomena, from dog whistles and hair growth to energy frequencies that vibrate at different dimensions of reality—including time dimensions. Occasionally these oddly different dimensions of reality seem to interphase with our own. A case in point took place in the early nineties when Frank and colleagues were investigating what may have been archaeological ruins at a small lake between Milwaukee and Madison, in southern Wisconsin.

It was a warm afternoon in late July. A member of the party, Jack Wayne Kennedy, skippered the group's pontoon boat toward the middle of Rock Lake. Frank was suiting up in scuba gear with help from Lloyd Hornbostel, a retired geologist.

Once they reached their destination on the lake, Frank flipped backward in his scuba gear and sank some thirty feet to the bottom. For almost an hour, he scoured the lake bottom for certain artifacts from antiquity.

Local Indians had historically revered the three-and-a-half-mile lake, calling it "Tyranena." They considered it a sacred site, due to the alleged presence of "rock teepees" on the bottom of it. According to legend, these were pyramidal structures that long ago belonged to a holy settlement before it sank entirely beneath the waves. Frank thought of these lost lake pyramids as a sort of Midwest Atlantis, lost beneath the waves of time.

Frank swam across a large expanse of the lake's bottom in his quest to explore the past but was unable to find any remnants of the lost Tyranena. With little air remaining, he rose slowly to the surface. He saw that his underwater search had taken him a fifth of a mile from the pontoon boat, where Jack and Lloyd had apparently lost track of his whereabouts given that there were no bubbles near their boat to spot him.

Once he had surfaced in his scuba gear, Frank said that he rolled over on his back and began to leisurely kick his way back to the boat with the clear blue sky overhead. Here is where his adventure took a surreal turn.

"I gradually began to hear," Frank recalls, "what I took to be the sound of a large crowd. Wrenching my head around to peer beyond my inflated vest, I craned my neck to get a better look at the eastern shore, about three-quarters of a mile away. That's where the disturbance seemed to be coming from."

Although he had a clear view across the tranquil water, Frank observed that Bartel's Beach was deserted. Still, the noise continued, increasing in volume. He determined that it was a large assembly of some kind with chanting or a singing group keeping time to music with a sort of ringing instrument that sounded metallic. Frank thought the ringing sounded like several metal plates loosely fastened to a staff that was being pounded on the ground. He said the clanging sound was in perfect time to the mass chanting he heard from afar.

"When I got within hailing distance of the pontoon boat," Frank recounts, "I called out to Lloyd: 'What's all that noise? What's going on at shore?'"

"Lloyd looked at me quizzically, but did not answer," Frank said. "By then, the chanting and zinging sound of some kind of percussion instruments was ever louder. But the moment my right hand grasped the boat's stern ladder, the noise fell abruptly silent, like a blaring radio suddenly yanked from its power cord."

After hauling himself on deck, Frank said he expected to see large crowds of celebrating people somewhere. But he saw none in any direction.

"Jack and Lloyd had neither seen nor heard anything," Frank said. "Although their denial seemed inexplicable, I assumed a sporting event of some kind must have taken place at a nearby football field in the neighboring town of Lake Mills. When we returned ashore, however, I learned that no public presentation of any kind had occurred in town that day. Nobody was playing a portable radio at either of Rock Lake's two beaches. There was no known source for the large mob I had heard."

Jack and Lloyd smiled upon hearing Frank's tale and seemed to think he was trying to fool them—at least initially.

"Later that evening," Frank recounts, "I had been invited to speak about Tyranena. At that meeting, a man said something rather revealing. He spoke up before I had an opportunity to describe my experience on the water that afternoon. . . . He claimed to have heard a crowd of Indian voices about the same moment that I heard chanting. He had been down at the north shore, about two miles from my position. He also failed to learn anything about the very vocal assembly. He asked me whether I might know anything about it."

Frank just looked at his companions, Jack and Lloyd.

They were no longer smiling.

Argument Overheard, Downers Grove, Illinois, 2007

Frank Joseph recounts one more personal account of a time shift that took place in the Chicago area. One summer evening in 2007 just before sunset, his Japanese American friend Kazume Kano was showing him a large estate in the western Chicago suburb of Downers Grove. The grounds had been abandoned after the owner of the estate had died. Kaz, a prominent customers' attorney, had been working hard to rescue its natural beauty from exploitation by developers. Lyman Woods is 150 acres of oak forest, original prairie, and marsh habitat that supports more than three hundred species of native plants as well as a variety of insects, birds, and other animal life.

"We walked its unmaintained paths for almost an hour," Frank remembers, "encountering no one. We were thoroughly satisfied that we were the only visitors. It was with some surprise, then, that we suddenly heard a man and woman arguing apparently nearby, but out of sight amid the thick foliage. Kaz and I stopped in our tracks and just stared at each other," Frank said. "The quarrel seemed to grow even more fervid. We could not make out what was being said, even though the voices seemed to come from no more than fifteen or twenty feet away. We were frozen in place, unsure as to what to do, until we heard a loud and distinct slap, as though delivered by an open palm to a cheek."

Frank's companion sprinted in the direction of the apparent attack. But he found nobody there. In fact, they discovered no sign that vegetation in that area had been disturbed by any intruders. Nor could they find any car in the preserve during their stay. The voices they'd heard seemed to have been entirely disembodied.

"We could never explain the experience," Frank said. "Although I suspect that our accidental presence at Lyman Woods triggered an audio document somehow stored in the environment—possibly a violent event that occurred there at a different time or in an alternate dimension."

EIGHT

Lucid Dreaming

The very fact that people can effectively program lucid dreaming to go back in time or forward in time by altering their consciousness makes me believe that people are capable of establishing portals *through* time.

When I wrote an earlier book on programming lucid dreams I was impressed by the number of responses I received from people who'd experienced verifiable precognition dreams and dreams in which they returned to a past that was not actually in their memory. Some of these reports came to me via radio phone-in shows from people who were amazed that they had actually visited other times and later had been able to verify the accuracy of what they'd learned.

Really, this shouldn't surprise anyone who knows anything about shamanic dreamwork or out-of-body Hindu meditation. In shamanic vision quests or spirit walking, the person goes into a state of altered consciousness and has vivid encounters in another time and place. The shamanic dream walking is often used for personal insight, while the shaman or holy leader of the tribe will seek to travel backward or forward in time to bring valuable direction back to his people. Similarly, samadhi mystics will go into deep trance-like meditations to travel outside normal time and space for personal growth and spiritual understanding.

At Panchavarnaswamy Temple, an ancient temple in India, one can see possible evidence of time travelers in sculpted stone figures of creatures believed to have roamed the Earth two thousand years ago as well as other mysterious creatures that nobody has yet seen on this planet.

The ancient Hindu text Bhagavata Purana describes time travel and quotes Lord Brahma as saying that time runs differently on different planes of existence. It would seem from visiting India's ancient temple of time travel that some early Hindu mystics have discovered this principle personally. In samadhi mysticism, the mystic voyager travels in a consciousness body, leaving the physical body carefully resting in peaceful repose. It would appear that none of the bodies physically disappear into another time and space but only project their consciousness there. There is the occasional reported sighting of an astral double, with the possibility of a doppelgänger, or dual functional entity of the same person, operating simultaneously. There are also stories of projected energy bodies that appear more solid and whole than what we consider to be astral doubles—and certainly more apparent than conscious bodies. That would be the case, it seems, with the Himalayan masters who were projected across great distances to visit people like Helena Blavatsky, Henry Olcott, and Alice Bailey. All three were early Theosophists who reportedly had personal encounters with advanced spiritual masters who remained otherwise secluded in the Himalayan Mountains. These masters were reported to be flesh and blood mortals and not ascended masters. It is assumed, therefore, that others could also master this technique of teleporting.

Nonetheless, it would seem that people encountered in time shifts do not readily see the drop-ins or respond to them. That would suggest that the interlopers are not customarily visible or physically present. This leads to the idea that these time travelers are projecting only their consciousness or energy body into the new time and space. There are conflicting reports about such blanket speculation, of course, if one considers the policeman in England who said the thief he was chasing seemed to disappear. Also, we must ponder reports from the Bermuda Triangle, where people, ships, and planes seem to physically disappear as well.

Of course, both scenarios could be true. We certainly know that people can project their conscious thoughts outside of themselves across space and time. On the other hand, people do seem to occasionally disappear and reappear.

For the vast amount of people who somehow experience time shifts and are not masters with special abilities, a simpler explanation probably exists to explain their random sidesteps into non-ordinary reality. This explanation would account for vivid, lucid, out-of-body dreams, precognition, past-life visits, and other escapes into another time and place. This explanation also might account for slips into energy vortexes, black holes, and singularities that seem to gobble up people from time to time and then spit them back out again.

I refer to a shift in consciousness in which the state of the higher consciousness aspect of what we commonly call our mind is altered to perceive things differently. That would also allow, possibly, for chemical or neurological changes in people to bring something like a black hole, singularity, power vortex, or escape hatch into their functional reality. Keep in mind that the experience of time shifts is very personal and seems to happen only to the individual when observers are not present. That would suggest that it's a controlled shift in perception, given that it doesn't involve others.

The scientific study of Masaru Emoto of Japan, author of *Hidden Messages in Water* and *The Healing Power of Water,* shows how even a group of children can project conscious thought to manifest real change in the world around them. In this study, Emoto explored the potential for water crystals to freeze in different shapes when exposed to varying thoughts, words, or music. This sort of manifested change is also proved by the Zen meditation experiments known as the Maharishi Effect, wherein a real world result can be seen in connection with a large number of people meditating simultaneously on that outcome. Clearly, shifts in our consciousness can manifest real change in the physical world around us.

Another way to consider the effect of consciousness to manifest perceived changes in our reality is to consider that space-time are dimensions not exclusively of our physical world but an added dimension outside of the control of laws of physics. It might then be logically suggested that one travels outside the physical body in an out-of-body vivid dream to another level of reality outside our three-dimensional reality. That is why I think of experiences like time slips or time shifts as personal sidesteps into a parallel plane of reality. Space-time, as we commonly perceive it, is likely not the same outside of our physical reality but rather more fluid.

It's hard to say where we go in our dreams when we examine our past in ways outside our memory or explore the future in precognitive dreams that come true in the course of regular, measured time. It seems likely that we do go somewhere outside our physical body and that the likely vehicle that takes us to some other space-time is our human consciousness.

Perhaps everything from an atom to the cosmos is infused and driven by consciousness, as Blavatsky and *The Book of Dzyan* insists. That would suggest that there is an underlying intelligence behind everything; an intelligence with the ability to reimage itself and things around us. It would suggest, as Charles Darwin hinted, that all conscious life purposefully directs its own evolution with conscious intent. If the physical side of Creation is really energy in a state of momentary repose, then it would follow that conscious intent could manifest changes on many levels.

Maybe, as poet William Ernest Henley said in his poem "Invictus," "I am the master of my fate; I am the captain of my soul." Maybe we *do* determine our own reality. Maybe we really *are* in charge of our own life and how it unfolds for us. Maybe the gods do *not* determine our fate but have placed us in a world that is ours to shape and reimagine.

I would prefer to believe that all of us are Odysseus on a challenging life journey of self-discovery, charting our own course. The course that I take might be different from yours. That would make all of us heroes of our life adventures. It would also make us larger than life with the ability to direct real change in the world as we see it.

John Milton in *Paradise Lost* wrote: "The mind is its own place, and in itself / Can make a Heav'n of Hell, a Hell of Heav'n." Maybe this world, this reality, is what we choose to make it—not with our hammers and brushes, but with the power of our consciousness to perceive and manifest change, moving between the worlds. The choices you make in your life are personal ones, not a group decision. Your dreams are not necessarily my dreams. Where you go and what you see is personally directed and perceived by you to determine your own reality. When your vision of reality becomes vivid, lucid, and fixed in your consciousness, it's safe to say that you have transformed your view of the world. And your view of the world becomes part of your moving reality, as you interpret and personalize the experience as meaningful reality for you.

Each one of us perceives the reality around us on a personalized level. No two people are likely to see something even as basic as the primary colors in exactly the same way. No two people necessarily agree on their interpretation of what they have seen. That doesn't necessarily invalidate anyone's observation as less than real.

With regard to the time shifts that many people claim to have experienced, there is little valuable empirical evidence to substantiate individual claims. Again, this is a personal journey of discovery. We have no scientific studies or statistical data to interpolate.

As we have mentioned, we do, however, have the inspired guidance of Albert Einstein, the Nobel Prize–winning physicist who studied space-time. He saw how time is perceived is differently by individual observers and must therefore be subjective by nature. He saw how time is dependent on the instant and on the location where light strikes what he called the "now" plane, initiating and validating *all* of life. As we read the mystical books that influenced Einstein, we see how Blavatsky viewed consciousness on a cosmic scale; it descends to the physical plane as radiant, everlasting light. Personally, I am comfortable with this scientist's interpretation of how we experience space-time. I believe that how we experience time is dependent on individual perception and measured by our consciousness. But I leave you to your own conclusions about how some people seem to experience the time shifts that they have trouble explaining to others. And you can decide for yourself what constitutes these sorts of time slips.

I would ask you to try a couple of personal exercises at this juncture to gain a feel for time and how we tend to experience it. Perhaps you can better evaluate things to your own satisfaction after these little meditations. They will stretch, test, and measure your consciousness.

With meditation we have a somewhat controlled method for placing someone in a state of heightened consciousness to enable that person to personally evaluate any shifts in the way the world is experienced, including that of time perception in the following exercise.

⑉➤Exercise: Perceiving Time

What's Needed

- loose-fitting, comfortable clothing
- the removal of shoes and socks
- the removal of jewelry, scarves, hat, or any other additional items that you might be wearing
- a quiet, secluded room where you can safely meditate without interruption
- a straight-backed chair or something like a pad, mat, or blanket on which to sit
- a very visible clock with a second hand that is easy to read, positioned right in front of you
- a watch with a second hand nearby, but not on your person

Procedure

Sit erect in a straight-backed chair or on a floor mat with erect posture and with your legs and arms extended and not crossed.

Your feet should be firmly planted on the ground.

Check the time on the watch or clock nearby to establish your starting time.

Clear your mind of any thoughts and tune out all external distractions.

Reach a quiet, still point deep inside yourself.

Focus your mind's eye on a blank slate in front of you and focus on it without any thought.

Begin deep controlled breathing and establish a rhythm of breathing in for three seconds, holding it for three seconds, and then exhaling it for three seconds. Continue this breathing pattern.

Slowly put your body to sleep, beginning with your toes and working your way up your body until you have consciously put your physical body to rest.

Now open your eyes and focus your gaze intently on the clock's sweeping second hand. With the full intent of your will, focus your conscious attention on stopping the second hand from advancing. As it moves forward, try to become one with the clock and inhabit the second hand. Focus your perception on the second hand intently and try to freeze it in place without advancing. This will become easier the more you focus your conscious intent.

Continue to focus your perception on the clock's second hand to stop the clock from advancing. Do not stop after only one or two attempts but continue to focus. If the second hand seems to stop or freeze in place and then advances, try to grab it again with your attention. Do this as long as you are able.

When you begin to feel exhausted, examine the elapsed time on the nearby watch or clock. Determine the exact time measured on the clock and compare it to the time you started. Did it seem that you were gone longer during this exercise than the amount of time actually measured on the clock? Did time seem to stand still with your focused attention?

How long did this exercise continue? Can you account for every second? Did it seem that you held back time? Did your focus on each passing second make time seem to last longer?

Note that this exercise measured your perception of time and did not impact the time passage or impression of time passing for anyone other than you.

This exercise might be somewhat familiar to any readers who have experience with yogic exercises as a training approach. It also is used in broader society to make people more conscious of time, and opens speculation that we really do hold the world together with our attention and can manifest changes in the plastic world of possibilities all around us.

The more you attempt this exercise, the more effective you are likely to become at seemingly stopping time or your perception of it.

⫸ Exercise: Lucid Dreaming

What's Needed

- a quiet, isolated room for private meditation
- a mat, blanket, or towel to place on the floor under you
- loose-fitting, comfortable clothing
- the removal of your shoes and socks
- the removal of your jewelry
- the removal of any hat or other exterior accessory with which you may be adorned
- a dream journal or pad with pen to write down your observations after the exercise

Procedure

Recline on your back on the mat or blanket with your arms and legs outstretched to a forty-five-degree angle. Do not cross your hands, feet, or fingers.

Slowly focus on consciously putting your physical body to rest, beginning with your toes and working your way up to the top of your head. Tell your body to rest and grow numb for the short duration of this exercise.

Tune out all external distractions, including your sensory observations, and then tune out all internal distractions, including your thoughts.

Begin deep regulated breathing and continue the pattern. Breathe in for approximately three seconds, hold that breath for approximately three seconds, and then exhale for approximately three seconds.

Go deeper and deeper inside your consciousness, where Spirit resides, to find a quiet, still point at your core.

When you feel that you have connected to your higher consciousness, focus your inner mind's eye on a clear slate in front of you.

On that clear blank slate begin to draw or paint a picture of your own design, of where you want to go. It can be anywhere and anytime of your choosing. Don't worry about the accuracy or detail of your drawing. It is only a simple map that will register with you on a deep personal level. It can even be a stick drawing or an abstract one. The point is that you comprehend the drawing as a map of where you plan to go.

Now tuck that drawing into the back of your mind to withdraw at a later time with the understanding that when you retrieve it you will automatically leave your body to go directly to that place of your choosing.

Give yourself permission to leave your body with the assurance that your physical self will remain safe and that you can easily return by simply focusing your consciousness on your physical location on the floor mat where you're reclining. You will automatically snap back, with a karmic attraction, to your body.

Now recall the drawing of where you want to go. When it appears on the blank screen in your mind's eye, you will automatically leave to visit that time and place.

When you are in this new time and place, take time to look

around and get your bearings. Note the colors and other details around you. Look at your hands to assure yourself that you really are in this new setting. Try to interact with your surroundings and observe any people you might see there.

When you return your conscious attention to your physical location on the floor mat in the meditation room, you will automatically snap back to that location.

Write your observations in your dream journal as soon as you have recovered and have had some quiet moments to reflect on what you've encountered.

This is an active, controlled dream. You could set up the parameters just before you go to sleep at night or set it up as a waking dream.

It is probably weighing on you whether your body remained behind in the room or just how much of you seemed to travel in your dream. You might have traveled in your consciousness, but your consciousness actually resides on all levels of your being, including your emotional or astral body, your mental body, your etheric double, your causal body, your Buddhic body of self-awareness, and your higher cosmic awareness body and godhead. Consequently, it is possible to focus on some or all of these subtle energy bodies that surround your physical body to take them with you. Doing so should make the encounter more enriching and increase your ability to be seen in this other time and space, if only as a phantom image. You might try to focus your intention on taking these energy bodies with you in the future.

Another improvement on this meditation exercise would be to set up a camera on yourself to record any detectible changes as you appear to travel from the meditation room. Did it seem to you that you really experienced a difference in space-time in your lucid, controlled dream?

This is one of the first exercises that samadhi mystics in India would attempt to master before they went on more elaborate astral voyages beyond mundane space and time. It is their belief that they can learn much and evolve as conscious beings by undertaking these astral voyages.

Is this time travel? You be the judge.

NINE

When a Dream Is More Than a Dream

Let's make some general assumptions here about our so-called dreams—universal truths that almost everyone can readily accept. There are various types of dreams. Some would appear to be simply memories and reflections that our subconscious keeps flashing before us like some old movie that has special meaning for us. These dreams seem to be the product of some effort of our brain to resolve problems, conflicts, or concerns that continue to trouble us—the sort of dreams that psychologists and psychiatrists often try to help us analyze and resolve.

Then there are dreams that seem all too real, vivid, and outside of our memory. These are not simple dreams. They seem to take us to new places of exploration and discovery. Often in these dreams, people find themselves miles away with a different set of people surrounding them and possibly in another time. We might call the process they're involved with active playful imagination, except that it seems too real and completely engages us to the point that we appear lost in time when we return to normal consciousness.

What seems to be different about the variety of dreams we experience is our level of consciousness when we are dreaming the dream. The subconscious mind, our lower mind, is that part of us that keeps dredging up problems and concerns that we try to hide somewhere down deep. But they keep bubbling up, as our subconscious mind releases the floodgates of our submerged memories. This is probably the brain trying to support the body's health and well-being by flushing out toxic thoughts, for our brain governs the routine functions of our physical body and looks after our survival.

Then we have those dreams that would appear to engage our higher consciousness. These so-called dreams seem to take us to places and times that we have not really explored before and times that we do *not* recognize as part of our memories.

Perhaps we should not call these experiences dreams at all, for it's true that people traditionally refer to anything that seems to happen in their mind as dreams or visions. It would appear that many of the places we go in our "dreams" at night when our physical bodies are asleep would be more than simple memories or internal conjecture.

The meditation exercise we recently participated in in the previous chapter sets up a waking dream. That is probably an inaccurate description, even though *waking dream* is a common label for a lucid dream that we experience while physically awake. Are we really dreaming during this waking dream or shifting our consciousness for visioning? I would submit that waking dreams, like many other things we tend to call our dreams, are not really dreams at all.

When we say we're dreaming—in the broadest sense, given the many kinds of activities we commonly call our dreams—we are using a cultural shorthand of sorts. This not only generalizes the activities involved but also tends to minimize them as imagination that happens only inside our head, with little significance other than inward reflection. In effect what we are saying, then, is that we were "only dreaming"—nothing more.

We tend to think of dreamers as sleepy-eyed, idle people who lie around and take little escapist journeys inside their heads. But this book is focused on bringing to your attention a possibility that not all of our dreams are simple memories or reflections, and not all of our journeys of this sort are necessarily limited to the space inside our heads.

What about those so-called dreams where you go somewhere you don't recognize and meet people you don't seem to know in your waking state? Where are you? Maybe, if you are like me, you find yourself returning to some unusual place and time night after night, developing an ongoing relationship with this place and time that is outside of normal space-time. I must confess that I have been leading a double life for years in this fashion, and perhaps you have as well. It would present as a parallel reality similar to the mundane world we inhabit physically.

I have been going there for years. And I know that I am not the only one. One of my first lucid adventures of this sort took me to a dark, rainy street corner of the town where I lived as a child. I found myself on Hewitt Avenue in Everett, Washington, when the buildings there looked very different. The people there were different, too. I noticed that there seemed to be no interaction of the people standing on the street in the dark rain. It was as though they were all sleepwalking and oblivious to their condition to some degree.

On one such adventure, I walked up to one of the men on the street and leaned into his face. It took him a long time to acknowledge me. He seemed startled to have this sort of interaction, as though he had been staring at a still landscape.

"Do you know that you are dreaming?" I asked him.

"What? What?" he blurted. Then he disappeared in front of my eyes. The other people on the street, equally oblivious, did not disappear, however.

If this sort of alternate reality experience makes me sound insane, then I will confess that I have been insane for years. I now know many of the people in this alternate reality and with a few of them I have an ongoing relationship that develops and evolves. As you probably realize, most simple dreams do not evolve or develop ongoing relationships but instead show us a static situation.

I have routinely experienced full adventures in a place and time that I only seem to visit in these lucid, vivid dreams. Sometimes they are waking dreams, but most often I will set up sleep time dream conditions so that I may leave the physical world behind and visit this exotic other world. It seems just as real and fulfilling to me as the mundane world that I experience during a normal day, maybe more so.

Because this is a world populated by people I do not commonly know and the world looks different from anyplace I recall from my waking experience, I would conclude that these dreams are not mere memories or idle reflections inside my brain. I don't think I have concocted this time and place out of pure mental imagination, since I interact somewhat with the people and environment in this alternate reality as though I have no personal control over the characters or setting.

It is telling, too, whether you have awareness in your so-called dreams. That would indicate that you are not just reprocessing memories but are actively engaged with heightened consciousness. We have all experienced enough recurring dreams and nightmares to realize that a simple dream as a subconscious memory does not allow one much freedom to act within the situation. Nor does it allow one to interact with the static props and characters that one confronts in these dreams.

Again, in these dreams, one is witnessing, not interacting. You try to move out of harm's way, but you are unable to move or to move quickly enough. You want to control the situation but seem to have little ability to do so. In the case of a recurring nightmare, you want a different outcome but seem to be on a roller-coaster ride without brakes or steering. It's like watching a movie and shouting for things to go a certain way, only to realize that it's only a two-dimensional recording that you're watching as an uninvolved observer.

You can probably give yourself some sort of posthypnotic suggestion to better cope with these nightmares. You may even try to sort out the internal problems that continue to haunt your dreams as troublesome memories. You could medicate reflectively on your nightmares and become your own best dream analyst, if you really tried. After all, nobody knows you better than you know yourself; thus, you should be able to interpret the symbolism and problems presented in your dreams.

But that's outside the scope of this book. We are looking here for dreams that are more than simple dreams of suppressed memories and suggest that some of what we commonly call dreams might be explorations into space-time shifts.

It's always amazing and inexplicable for many people when they dream about lost people or pets and seem to find them in their dreams. Either the lost find their way home shortly after these dreams transpire, or else the dreamer starts the new day with a hunch about where to start looking for them. We dream about what is important to us and what weighs heavily on our mind, so it is only natural for our super-consciousness to search for answers when released during peaceful repose. Our spirit cannot be denied and longs to roam and discover. For people or pets with whom we have a deep karmic connection, it is easy to see how our heightened consciousness leaps into action when our body and brain are asleep.

We also must remember the amazingly familiar stories of people who seem to dream the future only to see their visions come true in the light of day. It's almost as though they have visited the future and witnessed it for themselves. What other explanation could there be? Prophets have been called dreamers, and maybe that is close to the truth. Perhaps prophets do not simply forecast the future. Perhaps they travel to the future and bring back reports of what they have witnessed firsthand.

Many people enter a programmed dream state, as we commonly call it, to find themselves in a process that is called soul retrieval. The idea here is that you visualize going to a place where you believe you may have lost a key element of your essential being. Maybe it was at a time in your life when you became fragmented, so to speak. Maybe it was a place far away where a part of you was taken from you, leaving you emotionally, mentally, or spiritual incomplete and empty.

It is possible to set up a meditation to further explore this, much like a psychologist might use in hypnotherapy to return to a time and place in one's life when something went wrong. Returning to that time and place will allow you to confront the problem head-on to analyze what happened to you and perhaps strengthen yourself. If you have ever gone to such a distant place in your past, maybe it was not simply a memory but an actual journey. I think that's likely true, based on the fact that you are not simply reliving a memory but putting yourself into a picture and seeing it more clearly with mature eyes.

In a truly lucid dream that seems more than a recurrent memory or nightmare, people often report a greater, more heightened sense of awareness. This heightened sense is different from the five physical senses that people normally employ. Bruce Vance's book *DreamScape* notes how an active lucid dream is often distinguished by a whole new and different way of seeing, hearing, smelling, touching, hearing, and tasting. In fact, he reports that the lucid dreamer's senses are all turned upside down but are acutely focused. Outside our regular physical world, we do not have our normal five senses but are innately intuitive with a new awareness that only comes with a heightened consciousness of the spirit.

I would now like to introduce you to a meditation exercise that you can use to program yourself for an active lucid dream when you fall asleep. I need to confess something first, however. The first time I experienced a lucid dream, I did so accidentally. I fell back into my bed and triggered something when my spine struck the bed. I found myself dazed and drifting out of my physical body. It was perhaps similar to an accident wherein the spirit or consciousness instinctively evacuates a damaged body. I mention this to suggest that you don't need to program a lucid dream for when you fall asleep. You could put your body to sleep and enter a lucid dream *without* falling asleep. But programming a lucid dream and traveling outside normal time and space in a conscious body while you are reclining and peacefully asleep is a wonderful way to control your personal adventures into nonordinary time and space.

⇒ Exercise: Programming a Lucid Dream during Sleep

What's Needed

- a quiet, secluded room or place for you to meditate without interruption
- loose-fitting, comfortable clothing
- shoes removed
- jewelry, hats, and any other exterior apparel removed
- a mat, blanket, or towel suitable for you to recline on your back
- a little light that you can see when reclining on your back; natural light is best

Procedure

Recline on your back with arms and legs outstretched at forty-five-degree angles so that no hands, legs, or other parts of your body are crossing. This is to allow energy to flow in a clockwise fashion in your body without disruption.

Begin rhythmic deep breathing. Take a full three seconds to draw air into you with thanks. Then hold it inside you for a full three seconds with appreciation for the energy in it, and then expel it for three full seconds with your blessing for its future use. Continue this cycle until it begins to feel automatic.

Focus on the energy centers in the seven major chakras of your total body, recognizing that consciousness resides within your chakras in the subtle energy bodies that surround your physical self. Focus first on the red energy of the base chakra near the bottom of your spine. Then focus on the orange energy in the abdominal area, the yellow energy of the mental body higher up, the green energy in the heart area, the blue energy of the brow area, the indigo area of the forehead, and the violet flame above your head.

Open your eyes just a little to allow the light above you to filter past your eyelashes. At first you perceive only white light. Absorb and hold as much white light as you can and then intensify it.

Now consciously transform the white light into yellow light, building its intensity until it's bolder and brighter. Then transform the yellow light into orange light. Once you have intensified the orange light until it is bold, bright, and bouncy, transform it into red light. Once you have intensified the red from a pale red to a bold and energetic red light, transform it into a purple light. Consciously intensify the purple light from indigo to violet until it becomes a violet flame.

Now hold the full light inside you and close your eyes.

Focus your conscious attention on your physical body, beginning at your toes. Consciously put your feet to sleep, allowing them to become numb and restful. Then focus on putting your legs to sleep in this way, followed by your torso, chest, arms, and head. When you have put your nose, ears, and scalp to sleep in this fashion, your physical body should be totally at rest. This will allow you to go within yourself without physical distraction.

Now consciously tune out all external and internal distractions. Continue until no thought or words are going through your mind.

Next focus your mind's eye on a screen before you. The screen is lighted and energized, awaiting you.

On this screen, begin to draw or paint a picture of the location and time you want to travel to. This picture is a design of your own making and will become your perfect road map to take you to your destination when you are ready to leave your new destination.

Don't worry about the complexity of the picture you draw. It's just a simple blueprint that you will recognize. Once you see it again, you will automatically follow it like a map that only you can read. And because it's your personal design constructed with your own thought forms, it will be an accurate map for you and you alone.

Now take in the full scope of what you have drawn and prepare to tuck it away in the back of your mind, knowing that when you recall it you will follow it outside your physical body, beyond any physical limitations of ordinary time and space to the place and time you have selected.

Tuck it away in the back of your mind and prepare yourself for the journey ahead. Give yourself full permission to leave your body with the assurance that it will be safe and rested when you leave and that you will be able to return to it once you have visited your destination by simply projecting your consciousness back to it.

Visualize a screen, like a TV screen, in front of you now. If you are programming yourself for a waking dream, then proceed directly by immediately recalling the picture you just drew to the screen in front of your mind's eye. Follow that image to the place you have determined.

If you are setting up a controlled sleeping dream, then you allow yourself to drift off to sleep with the conscious thought as a planted suggestion that you will automatically return to your designated road map when your lower conscious mind gives way in sleep mode. Fall asleep with this conscious intent. In this way, you have programmed a controlled dream outside of your body.

When you are ready, you will automatically recall the picture to the screen in front of your mind's eye and follow the image to the place you have determined.

When you are there, look around to take in everything, noticing the colors and details. Look at your hands to recognize that you have taken subtle energy bodies with you and that you have nonphysical form.

Analyze what you come to study and understand. If you are visiting a prior or future version of yourself, then you might project energy to yourself there to strengthen your mental, emotional, spiritual, or causal body. It's alright to relate to yourself in this way.

All you need to do to return easily and safely to your physical body in the meditation room is to shift your conscious focus back to your physical body. You will naturally snap back into it. The entire trip outside yourself and back to the room can be instantaneous.

Once you are back, continue to recline on your back and quietly meditate on what you have observed. Once you have analyzed the experience and reflected on it, then slowly allow physical sensation to return to your body, beginning again with your feet and working your way up your body. When you feel fully back in your body, slowly open your eyes and adjust yourself before attempting to sit up.

Allow yourself some quiet time before rising to internalize what you have experienced and what it has meant to you. What you have seen and felt might be hard to assimilate within your frame of reference at first. This is a deeper way of looking at things. It would be easiest to discard them as fanciful visions, since they might not coincide with the way you have previously viewed things. But trust the insights that you have been shown. They are your personal observations.

It might help the analytical side of you to write your observations in a notebook after this exercise.

TEN

Experiencing Time and Different Dimensions

There is little denying that how we experience time is based on our perception. It depends largely on where we are standing, the conditions of the encounter, and our own subjective relationship to the flow of events. Not everyone, it would seem, experiences time in exactly the same way or senses time passing at the same rate.

First, we are three-dimensional creatures with five physical senses that we utilize as a primary means of defining the reality around us. We think in linear terms with everything starting at one point and following forward in one straight line to a terminal point.

So, it was naturally shocking to many of our ancestors that the world was round. Movement in any direction in a straight line naturally led us around the world and ultimately back to the point of origination. There are few "flat earthers" among us today, now that explorers in boats and planes have circumnavigated our physical world. The sad truth, nonetheless, is that few people think with any real depth, and the rest see the world in only two-dimensional parameters.

As humans, it seems that we can only relate to what we can see, hear, feel, touch, or taste. We cannot relate to dimensions that we do not perceive. There could be an unlimited number of diverse realities near us that are beyond our ability to perceive. It is like living on one level of a building with a ceiling above us and a floor below us that prevent us from hearing, seeing, or otherwise perceiving anything above or below. So that becomes the limitation of our world.

As philosopher P. D. Ouspensky, a colleague of Gurdjieff, argued in his book *Tertium Origanum,* we cannot perceive the world above the level where we live as three-dimensional beings. Ouspensky postulated that one-dimensional beings on a level below us could not relate to us either. The only way we might experience other dimensions and other realities, he suggested, is to raise our consciousness to see with new eyes and hear with new ears in a state of heightened consciousness. This is familiar to yogi mystics and shamanic visionaries perhaps, but it is beyond the experience of most people.

What exists beyond the limits of our three dimensions, very likely, are multiple worlds and multiple realities, which is what cutting-edge physicists now suggest. It is like folds in a carefully folded map that we cannot peek around. We can only speculate at the unseen parts of the folded map.

A few of us, however, might accidentally sidestep into these alternate realities, most likely in an altered state on a day when we somehow experience a shift in consciousness that allows us to see with new eyes and hear with new ears, as is also suggested in the Holy Bible. That would give these people a different perspective.

I suspect that you have worn sunglasses at one time or another and as a result experienced the world around you in a different way. Or maybe you have worn 3-D glasses at the movies and saw things that you would not be able to see without them. Maybe, too, you have worn night-vision goggles that allow you to see in the dark. Surely, you may have looked through binoculars or a scope that allowed you to perceive things that were otherwise oblivious to you in the broad world around you.

Sometimes we call glasses "cheaters," because they give us an advantage over our naked eyes. Even people with good eyes often use reading glasses, magnifying glasses, or microscopes when necessary to penetrate beyond their normal vision. There is much to see and experience beyond the limitations of our five physical senses.

Our view of the world around us and our view of reality is rather dark and dim, if you weigh our physical gifts of perception. We cannot see nearly as well as an eagle or most of the millions of various birds that fill our skies. Even on the ground without a bird's-eye view of things, we score low when it comes to what we can perceive. For instance, we do not see nearly as well as a cat, and we do not hear nearly as well as a dog.

Many other animals who share our world seem to have perceptive skills that we do not possess. If you have ever tried to "squirrel-proof" a bird feeder or tree so that squirrels could not have access to it, you realize how little animals who live in nests can outmaneuver us so easily. They seem to have inherent abilities of perception that we do not understand. It is simply beyond our points of reference and the range of our ability.

Surely you may have been as amazed as I have to see large flocks of birds quite suddenly change direction when they all detect something that is oblivious to us humans. Surely, too, you have noticed how birds and other animals seem to sense when a huge storm or immediate danger is coming. Can they see into the future? Do they have senses that we don't possess, or do they simply have keener senses?

I would suggest to you that people have been cultivated through social interactions throughout the ages to live inside our little analytical brains. This is the lower mind that we utilize to make tools, plot interactive strategy, and practice the one-upmanship that seems to preoccupy most people most of the time. What we lack is situational awareness, because we are preoccupied inside our heads—where we live and where we hide with our petty thoughts.

We have chosen to lock ourselves inside our boxes, thereby keeping us separate and apart from everything outside of what we can easily see and hear. We have subjugated ourselves to cultural training that develops our analytical brain and ignores our higher consciousness. That higher consciousness is precisely what allows a being to think outside the box in which we find ourselves.

Other animals, it would seem, have not spent so much time cultivating the analytical mind and live more in the moment, open to the possibilities of a broader view of reality. They have great situational awareness.

I still shake my head in disbelief when I recall the amazingly perceptive skills of some of my former pets. I'm certain that if you have lived with pets then you can recall similar feats with your own pets; often they seem to perceive things in ways we cannot.

The Three-Hundred-Mile Cat Walk

I once had a tortoise-shell-colored cat named Mildred, who was named after our amazing postmaster in Petersburg, Alaska. Mildred the cat traveled across the country with me after I left Alaska. She wouldn't leave my side. I could pull into a roadside motel in the middle of nowhere and leave the door to my room open so she could go outside and roam. In the morning, she would return to the room or else be waiting on the hood of my old Ford Bronco. She had a tremendous homing instinct.

That instinct was put to the test finally when I left her with my family in Marysville, Washington, for a few weeks. After some time, Mildred disappeared from Marysville, and she was gone for a long time.

Then she appeared at my brother's place in Eugene, Oregon, several weeks later. I had never taken Mildred there, but she knew my brother. And I had been to his home there. The cat appeared one day at his front door and meowed in her distinctive way when she saw him.

That suggests that Mildred walked due south for many hundreds of miles, crossing rivers, bridges, and high-traffic areas. Once you are walking on Interstate 5, I would note, it would be hard to make a hard left turn up Mount Hood after crossing the bridge over the raging

Columbia River. I assume that Mildred walked on I-5 south, since the idea of a small house cat swimming across the mighty Columbia is a bit hard to imagine, even if the cat was a determined little feline.

Mildred might have been following a scent trail to my brother's door. Or maybe she had another way of dead reckoning her way. I know from my limited flight training in southeast Alaska that a human's sense of dead reckoning is limited. The one time I had to follow my flying instincts to find Petersburg in a low fog bank, without instruments, I nearly crashed our little plane onto the top deck of the state ferry. It was parked exactly where I thought our landing zone might be. It was not a good approach, as the shocked passengers on the MV *Wickersham* would testify.

My Alaskan cat, Mildred, was distinctive in color, personality, and voice. My brother recognized her instantly. She walked right up to him as though she knew him. Then she scoped out the place and left abruptly. None of us ever saw her again. She never returned to my brother's house, probably because she did not find me there.

I would like to say that Mildred was a superior example of what a cat can be, but I know she was not unique. There are many documented stories of dogs—household pets with little experience outside on their own—who traveled tremendous distances over time to find their homes or their human companions. Surely you have heard one or more such story.

Birds seem to have that sort of homing device, too. Pigeons were once used to deliver messages across great distances, using a sense we seem to lack in great measure. Other birds can navigate their way around the world. Whales can do that, too, and have the added ability of being able to communicate from ocean to ocean across the vast expanse of the planet.

It would appear on the surface that these incredible animals who share this physical world with us have a greater sense of situational skills than people do. Maybe we had these skills when we were primitive creatures and lived more closely in harmony with the forces of nature, but our culture has somehow driven this greater situational awareness out of us. In our societies of today, we have shielded ourselves in the solitude of our thoughts.

If so, our similar abilities must be present as latent powers, although we do not normally utilize them in the same way as a cat, of course. Perhaps these latent abilities are possible to cultivate as extrasensory perceptive skills. The existence of psychics among us seems to suggest that this is a human possibility. No doubt you've heard of telepathy wherein we can send our thoughts around the world in a flash. Many people have experienced this sort of instantaneous communication. Our thoughtforms leave our body at what may seem to be the speed of light. They are energized consciousness projected from us with focus and intent.

Perhaps in this way you have experienced sending thoughts to people who are close to you. Or maybe you have been on the receiving end of a telepathic message. We must forget thinking about telepathic thought as something imaginary or simply lore, for it's not something that happens to a few strange people with active imaginations. It happens to all of us throughout the course of any given day, although most of us seem unwilling to believe in the validity of the process. That's probably because we cannot measure it with our three dimensions and reduce it to linear thinking with the typical mind-set of a material reductionist.

The Same Cat Could See around Corners

Mildred's stay at my parents' home in Marysville, Washington, provided me with many stories that demonstrate the conscious awareness of animals. One of my favorite Mildred stories is how she could see around corners. Or at least that is the way it seemed to me.

She would explore the rafters in the upstairs bedroom where I would stay when visiting my parents. The rafters were constructed in the attic and were like a maze of dead-end passages. A person would have been completely lost in these tunnels where she roamed, for it was completely dark, with no cracks or holes to see through or past the wooden boards. Sometimes I would call for her to join me in the room. That did not necessarily get her back into the bedroom, however, because she would enter a dead end and just meow back at me from the other side of the wall.

Once she really amazed me, however, doing something I did not consider possible. On this occasion, I failed to recognize that she had entered the maze of rafters. I should have known better, given that the attic trapdoor was open, but again I did not notice that. Like most cats, Mildred was a born explorer and set out on her own in dark places without much notice or concern.

I was alone in the bedroom for quite some time before I started to wonder about my cat, not having seen her in some time. I went downstairs and looked around. I asked whether anyone had let her outdoors and determined that nobody had seen her in a while.

So, I returned upstairs and then realized that I had left the attic door open. I wondered if she was in there but decided that since I had been in the bedroom with the door closed, she could not have come into the room to go up into the rafters again. Of course, it did not occur to me that she had been in the rafters for hours before I'd ever entered the room, wandering around in that maze of dead-end passages. So, I just ignored the issue for a while, hoping she would appear out of nowhere later that night when it was time for her meal.

Then I heard a weak, pathetic meow from the attic doorway. She must have found her way through the maze to an area near my room, despite the lack of peepholes, light, or sound to guide her. She had reached the point where the attic rafters dead-ended at the doorway to my bedroom. When she meowed to get my attention, I knocked on the board that separated us. She scratched at it from the other side in response. I then pried off the board to allow her to enter the bedroom.

She bounced happily into the room, seemingly both anxious and relieved. She swatted at me as though to complain that I'd taken too long to help her. She had known where I was, after all, and apparently couldn't understand why I hadn't been able to locate her.

This incident rather upends the old myth that animals are not abstract thinkers. To be an abstract thinker, one would need to be able to imagine something beyond what one can see with the naked eye. You would need to imagine the room on the other side of the attic wall, just as Mildred evidently did.

I recall taking photographs years ago as a young staff member of the newspaper in Anacortes, Washington, at that seaside town's first outdoor summer arts festival. I was roaming around with a camera that August weekend and noticed a dog hiding from someone on the other side of an upright mirror on the street. I think the idea was to examine yourself in the mirror while wearing a hat or scarf made by the exhibitor. A lady was looking into the mirror, while the artist at that exhibit was looking for his dog.

The dog, however, was standing in a guarded position, crouching behind the mirror. He was looking into the back of the mirror, obviously aware of people on the other side of it who could see only their reflection. *A sly dog,* I thought, as I snapped my photograph.

I had a personal experience with my sly cat who seemed able to see or imagine what was behind a wall. This animal sense is a different kind of vision from what most people seem to exhibit. People traditionally refer to such animal stories, I suppose, as examples of animal cunning or instinct. Deer know when to hide when the hunting season begins. Birds know that a storm is coming before there are any visible signs of it. Dogs are used today as therapy pets to predict when human companions will have seizures before the seizures begin.

These animals have a conscious awareness that we do not seem to possess. We rely on our weak physical senses and our obsession with measuring everything in a two-dimensional, linear fashion. Other animals seem to master these abilities and more. They are not preoccupied, as we are perhaps, with their analytical thoughts and compulsions about trying to control a situation by quantifying things in simple measurements they can comprehend. They allow themselves to reach out with a heightened consciousness that operates outside of themselves.

We must remember that consciousness is not composed of mere brain calculations or mental reflections. It's instead an awareness or connectedness that exists on a nonphysical level. Consciousness permeates the cosmos, propelling and sustaining all of life everywhere, from the heavens above to every aspect of the world below. It is carried by the electromagnetic energy that rains down upon our world in radiant light. Electromagnetic energy initiates and activates all of life, bringing it into conscious awareness. If you stand outside in the open air on a sunny day, you immediately feel the energy. You do not feel that inside the box where you live much of your life.

This consciousness exists on every chakra level of our subtle energy bodies that surround our physical form, giving us root energy, emotional energy, causal energy, mental energy, psychic energy, and spiritual energy. Animals like cats, dogs, horses, birds, and whales don't need to study any of this. They know it instinctively because they are in touch with their total being, living outside of boxes and outside of their heads.

If we could reach this level of open, situational awareness and employ our heightened consciousness, perhaps we would not feel so restricted. Perhaps the limitations of our physical world and the laws of physics would not hold us back.

What people who sidestep outside normal time and space seem to notice is that they find themselves in a slightly shifted frame of mind. Perhaps altered perception comes with an altered consciousness in which our little, analytical brains tune out and our heightened consciousness shifts us to new levels of awareness beyond ordinary time and space.

In the East, mystics who enter deep meditations out of the body seem to do precisely that and have done so for hundreds of years. So, too, shamanic visionaries seem to walk beyond normal time and space when in a trance state. There are examples around the world of people who can do this. We sometimes call these people special or gifted. Maybe, though, everyone has this potential.

ELEVEN

The East's Approach to Time Travel

Time travel does not seem odd or controversial to many serious students of deep meditation in the East. Yogi masters and their students have been practicing it for hundreds of years as a disciplined training. It is particularly well known in samadhi mysticism, but familiar to anyone who has studied the more magical and mystical sections of the ancient guide to meditation, *The Yoga Sutras of Patanjali*. Hindu and Buddhist meditation students alike are undoubtedly aware of this classic yoga book. The first part of *The Yoga Sutras of Patanjali* contains basic meditation exercises. Mystical and magical meditations are included in later sections, which most people probably never reach.

In the West, people often think of yoga as stretching exercises, given that hatha yoga introduces new students to postures and physical forms to discipline the body. People in the West are just beginning to see the health benefits of yoga to reduce stress, improve circulation, and improve breath control.

Yoga seeks to bring one in harmony or unity with all of Creation and not simply tone the physical body. And when one reads deeper into *The Yoga Sutras of Patanjali,* this lofty goal seems realistic on a personal level.

Advanced meditation exercises explore reality, consciousness, and transformation. The dedicated yogi could expect, with focus and dedication, to master these deeper meditations so as to examine the nature of reality and alternate realities. In these deep, active meditations, one could explore the depth of consciousness and altered states of consciousness. The focused yogi could even expect personal transformation.

Hence, the mystical and magical levels of meditation could take advanced students beyond the ordinary experience of fixed time and space in a restricted physical world and all of its limitations. At least these advanced students claim to experience a sense of being outside mundane space-time. They report going to other places and times on the Earth plane as well.

The renowned author and teacher Paul Twitchell, founder of Eckankar—the science of soul travel—was inspired by a Hindu master named Kirpal Singh who could travel outside normal time and space in this fashion.

Twitchell described many of his spiritual voyages to other realms of creation in these deep meditations. He was one of several masters of Eastern mysticism who developed this mastery of time and space through meditation.

Nada Yoga and the Upanishads

Kirpal Singh was a master in a long line of yogi mystics who followed a spiritual practice known generally as surat shadba yoga, or sehaj yoga, the path of sound and light and the journey of the soul. This discipline's basic approach involves the discovery of the true self (self-realization), true essence (spiritual identity), and divinity. Students practice various exercises to reunite with the supreme being.

This approach to yoga arose in India hundreds of years ago and is based on spiritual exercises from the Hindu practice of nada yoga as described in the ancient scriptures known as the Upanishads and the even older *Rig-Veda*. Nada yoga has been important to such Eastern notables as Swami Sivananda, Swami Rama, and Paramahansa

Yogananda, as well as to Tibetan mystics and many Sikhs. Helena Blavatsky's classic book *The Voice of the Silence* is a good primer on this basic approach. Originating in the East, nada yoga combines elements from the Hindu practices of raja yoga, laya yoga, and bhakti yoga and has inspired millions worldwide.

The chela, or student, learns to develop and accelerate personal perception by focusing concentration on an object or sound, progressing from sensing only that object or sound to seeing *beyond* that object or sound. Given that our understanding of reality is based on what we believe we see, hear, or otherwise perceive with our physical senses, the key is to better develop those perceptive skills as well as to enhance them. Thus, we may see beyond the illusion of our physical world of energy, which is always in a fluctuating state given the ever fluid state of matter.

Adherents are likely to discover inner sound and light as well. A deeper understanding of inner sight, inner hearing, inner vibration, and an advanced sense of taste and smell overlays the basic sensory perceptions. The practice is meant to turn these keener senses inward to experience an inner self.

The Samadhi Mystic

The samadhi mystic goes into a trance-like state to reach a higher state of meditative consciousness. The approach is practiced in Hinduism, Buddhism, Jainism, and Sikhism. In this form of meditation, the practitioner becomes absorbed in the meditation and develops a more luminous mind. It is the eighth limb in *The Yoga Sutras of Patanjali* and the last of the eight elements in Buddhism's Noble Eightfold Path.

In samadhi mysticism, the student reaches four meditative states, often considered formless dimensions. In this practice, one reaches infinite space, infinite consciousness, infinite nothingness, and a new experience of perception.

It is said in Buddhism that when a monk has developed higher knowledge through the practice of meditation, he can open a realization to witness what others cannot experience. Furthermore, he can exhibit supernormal powers as he becomes one with all and reaches spiritual unity. He can appear, vanish, walk unimpeded through walls, and traverse mountains easily. He can dive in and out of the earth, walk on water, fly through the air like a bird, and stroke the surface of the sun and moon. Through deep meditation, he finds an opening to see all of this and experience all of this.

Curiously, the first thing that many samadhi students will practice is control over their dreams wherein they experience and acknowledge a power over time and space as they travel in their controlled dreams with conscious awareness. Interested people in the West have explored something similar with lucid dreaming and dream journaling, although without the typical discipline and focus of samadhi students, who understand that they are exploring alternate realms and realities. This is compatible, I would suggest, with cutting-edge physicists in the West who describe the viability of a *multiverse,* or a complex universe with parallel worlds and realities that are somehow oblivious to the casual observer. Indeed, there could be multiple universes.

Samadhi mystics go into such deep and active meditations that they consciously experience leaving their physical bodies as energy bodies and leaving the space and time in which their reclining physical bodies lay quietly. I have taken Western students on long workshop retreats into deep meditation wherein they leave their body in this way and experience time shifts. They would reach states so deep that they didn't stir, cough, blink, twitch, or show any apparent indication that they were aware of the room in which they reclined on their backs. They would remain in this state for hours and hours and it would actually prove very difficult to bring them out of this deep, meditative state once they had determined a destination and left their physical bodies. It would take some time as an outside guide to return them to the room and normal consciousness inside their bodies in the here and now.

I would point out that this workshop group included many people who had no or relatively little previous meditation training. They were realtors, teachers, dentists, photographers, and other curious, open-minded spiritual seekers. Some of them believed that such spiritual voyaging was impossible and did not expect the experience of deep out-of-body consciousness that, much to their surprise, they encountered.

I recall that on one occasion I left them in the meditation room and walked around the building and through the trees at a weeklong retreat at Omega Institute of Holistic Studies in Rhinebeck, New York. I kept returning to the room to physically check on things, but nobody seemed to be coming out of their deep, meditative state.

All of these individuals had selected a specific time and place that they wanted to visit and focused their heightening consciousness on leaving the room to visit that particular place and time. They were determined to explore and discover various concerns of personal interest to them. All of them had a karmic investment and attachment to the journey they had programmed.

Some journeys are complicated. Sometimes a distant horizon needs to be studied carefully and in depth to interpersonalize the impact and significance of what one might encounter there. We come with preconceptions that will be challenged as we see with new eyes and hear with new ears in what is often a voyage of discovery. This sort of journey cannot be hurried; change on this level takes as long as it takes. Transformation is not simply flipping a switch but instead learning to change and adapt to the experience and the changes it may bring as part of our personal growth.

My point is that all people can learn these techniques if they apply themselves. One simply needs to be willing to grow and change, which is often a by-product of any open-ended adventure.

My favorite story about the depth and focus of samadhi mystics is a story of Hindu chelas who had undergone deep meditation just before a huge storm and its tsunami swept across southern India and Indonesia a few years ago. People worried about the chelas, who were engaged in deep, trance-like meditations at the time. People were also worried, however, about disturbing them and didn't want to wake them, despite the pressing storm.

It was considered unsafe and improper to disturb them when they were in the extreme depth of their meditation, considering how far out some of them were. The ideal situation, it was determined, was to allow them to resurface on their own when their spiritual voyages were complete. (That probably explains a little why I found it hard to get my realtors and dentists to resurface back at our retreat in New York. Maybe I shouldn't have tried!)

Their friends did not even try to wake them to escape the storm. They carefully wrapped them in warm blankets and carried them away to safety. Days later they awoke from their deep meditation in a totally different place, safely removed from the storm that had battered the coast. They were completely unaware of the move and apparently not conscious of any of the efforts that had been taken to protect their physical bodies.

Ordinarily, people who enter a meditative state of any depth are carefully tucked away and not touched by others. In fact, people who surrender their physical bodies to rest and quiet solitude during meditation normally consider it a prerequisite to have this sort of privacy without any interaction.

Contrasting the depth of the samadhi chelas in the storm's way in southern India with my novice students in deep meditation at Omega Institute is not a fair comparison, perhaps. But it does suggest something about the focus of the serious samadhi when compared with the weekend workshop participants at Omega in the West, as determined as my students were.

The samadhi mystics who submerged themselves in such deep voyages outside the body, unaware of the storm facing their physical bodies, had induced their own trance-like states without a guide. My Omega students, on the other hand, were following the prompts of a guide; namely, me. I had helped them to enter a deep, out-of-body meditation. Consequently, I still exercised some control over them and could awaken them with my voice when our weeklong workshop drew to a close on that final day.

Ideally, you can become the own master of your soul and captain of your fate without a guide to put you out there and call you back. In a true voyage of discovery and adventure, a hero sets course with a personal sense of direction, not certain where the winds may lead but willing to undergo the challenges of the path ahead. This is a path without markers and without guides, for nobody can direct you. You are willing to face the storms that might beset you from any direction in your quest for growth and understanding. And as your reward, you become one with the elements and the cosmos in ways that were only mysterious before. Along the way, you discover your true self and your greater potential as you stretch your consciousness to heights you never imagined back home, safe in your easy chair.

As the Indian sage J. Krishnamurti once told his students, "Truth is a pathless land."

TWELVE

The Shamanic Experience of Time Travel

Eastern mystics are not the only sizable group of people who experience non-ordinary space-time. Another group of people are shamanic visionaries.

Shamanism is sometimes considered to be the origin of all organized global religions. It is essentially folk spiritualism and as such has guided and inspired people around the world. Shamanism unites people through trance, ritual, songs, and storytelling with spirits, ancestors, and elements of nature around them, encouraging them to forge a symbiotic relationship and spiritual bond with the earth, water, and sky. In this earth-based spirituality people typically honor and respect the forces of nature—from wind to rain and fire. Shamanism has typically arisen among indigenous or native people, a designation indicating that they are not world explorers, migrants, or nomads but are instead tied to the land where they and their ancestors were born. As a result, they are concerned about the care of the land, waterways, and sky, given that they seek to preserve their habitat for future generations who, it is expected, will live there also. Shamanism itself, in fact, is also found all over the world, despite the encroachment of civilization into the rural settings where it often originated. Across cultures, this type of spirituality served an important social role, and, as we'll see, may even have taken the shamans through time.

There were a wide number of indigenous tribes in North America, with spiritual values and practices varying from one tribe to another. North American indigenous people honored spiritual leaders with various designations. Typically, they would refer to that individual as the medicine man of the tribe, a ritual leader, or even the keeper of tribal lore. The medicine man would summon spirits for healing and recite the legends of the tribe in their oral traditions.

The term *shaman* comes from Siberian languages but was and still is often applied to these native North American holy men; they are true visionaries in the shamanic tradition, and the term has since been expanded to refer to the ritual leaders of many different folk spiritualties. Special women among these people are often designated as community medicine women. They work with the herbs of the Earth to sustain and restore the health of the people. Beyond North America, of course, we see many other examples of the shamanic tradition wherein these indigenous people use trance in a religious context and live in harmony with the elements and forces of nature around them. This includes indigenous people of the islands in the Pacific to natives in Australia, as well as African and Atlantic tribes, and Montagnards in Southeast Asia.

Shamanic people of the Hawaiian Islands sometimes call themselves "children of the rainbow." Using an instrument called the *ohe hano ihu,* a traditional nose flute, they play music to contact and communicate with nature. They believe that spirits in the volcanoes speak to them. They are one with their land and the spirits of the land, sky, and sea.

Africa has many shamanic traditions, including those of the Zulu tribes of South Africa. Various African shamanic traditions have spread across the world as far west as the Caribbean and into the deep South of the United States. Afro-Caribbean shamanism is alive and well today. Most notably, it can be found in Puerto Rico, Florida, and other relocation points of Cuban Americans, such as New York City.

An early African shaman from Mali, according to ancient folklore, came under the control of fairies and was kept prisoner by them. It was during his captivity that he learned their fairy magic and became skillful in using it on his own. Tribal shamans in Mali today treat their people like a flock under their care and supervision in keeping with this ancient shamanic tradition. In fact, their tribal shamans are their religious leaders in all social situations. Consequently, their influence in this role is rather broad and far-reaching.

Indigenous people in Australia live close to the land and the spirits of the land even today, despite modern society crowding in on them. They are famous for their "walkabouts"— spiritual sojourns across the vast expanse of their large continent.

The Hmong people of China are another ancient indigenous group within the shamanic tradition. They practice spiritual healing; and in their tradition, all souls are interchangeable. The shaman as holy leader of the tribe speaks to the gods on behalf of the people. Animal souls are considered interchangeable with the souls of people. The soul of a person could inhabit another animal, and the soul of an animal could inhabit a person in this shamanic tradition.

American soldiers in Vietnam in the 1960s were amazed to find reclusive mountain people, called "Montagnards" by the French during their own occupation of the area. These people practiced animism, which reflected sensitivity to nature and the belief that spirits were present and active in the natural world. They recognized both good and bad spirits and practiced rituals to appease the spirit world.

Mongolian shamanism, common even today, calls upon the good spirits for healing and guidance. This again is the role of the shaman. He calls down the rain, drives out evil spirits, and summons spirits for healing and guidance for the people he leads.

Surviving Christian conversion, Siberians practiced shamanism until they were subject to Communist persecution from Russians who tried to halt all religious practice in the twentieth century. Siberia had until that time practiced a daily connection to the world of Spirit in the true shamanic tradition. Siberia, in fact, has been considered the heartland of shamanism by many researchers. Shamans in Siberia would go on a spirit-journey to rescue the soul of one of their people or find the soul in a controlled dream. They would also heal in séances. In many parts of Siberia, old shamanic practices continue today.

Indigenous people in Papua, New Guinea, and elsewhere in Oceania also followed a form of folk spirituality under the leadership of a shaman. A common belief was that illness was caused by dark spirits that would attach themselves to a person's body to drain their health. A principal role of the shaman in these cultures, then, was to help an afflicted person drive away the evil spirits. Shamans also guided the hunt by leading the people in rituals that enabled them to access more food. Shamans would perform rain ceremonies to bring rain to the crops as well. Shamans in these places also served the somewhat unusual function of maintaining tribal law through enforcement and punishment. They would put a hex on anyone who broke the laws of the tribe.

In South America, shamanism has a long history in the Amazonian and Andean regions, where indigenous people relied on spirit healers called *curanderos*. These healers turned to the Earth for herbs and other natural remedies of the land. They also designed charts with classifications of herbs to guide them in curing specific types of illnesses. Their shamans were legendary for controlling weather and driving out evil spirits, and they would appear as a spirit animal in costumed attire whenever they spoke to the gods of the spirit realm.

Indigenous people of the Amazon believe in "soul flight" in which shamans would go into a visionary trance and visit good spirits beyond our immediate realm for help in healing. This tradition continues even today to some degree, as people along the Amazon River use these same shamanic remedies to treat everything from the common cold to the most life-threatening forms of cancer.

Mesoamerican tribes have much in common with North American indigenous peoples, including common origins and history in some cases. As with North American shamanic peoples, Mesoamerican culture featured a wide variety of religious diversity and ceremonies.

These tribes included the famous civilizations of the Mayans and Aztecs, which were powerful and bloody shamanic cultures. Mayans looked to the stars and other heavenly bodies to help them interpret the future. Many people are perhaps familiar today with the Toltec tradition of shamanism described by anthropologist and novelist Carlos Castaneda, but there are many other examples going back to pre-Columbia times with the Mayans and the Aztecs. Even today, we can see in the Huichol tribe of west central Mexico the continuation of an ancient shamanic tradition rooted in the pre-Columbia era. There, shamans as guides into the spirit realm heal and lead their people, who honor the old ways without electricity but with great reverence for nature as provider.

Bloodletting rituals were common practice in Mesoamerican shamanic tradition, particularly among the Mayans. The blood often was seen as an offering to the gods. There was also a traditional belief that one could see into the future through a divination of the blood flow in one's veins. They would determine the pattern of the pulse in the human body and then study it to interpret the future.

There were many European shamanic traditions, and some continue today, particularly in Eastern Europe. Many of these European traditions are thought to be based on the practices of the Druids—the forest priests and healers of the ancient Celts, who date back to the third century. The Druids served many functions, including that of soothsayer, teacher, magician, and judge.

Shamanism's Legacy with Trances and Time Shifts

In many ways, shamanism is alive and well today, for the spiritual traditions of our ancestors continue to play a part in modern society around the world. One defining characteristic of the shamanic tradition, of course, is the attainment of insights through trance-like visions. That legacy is valuable to us and important to our discussion about time shifts here.

The shaman's shift in consciousness would put him into a deep, trance-like state wherein he would appear to lose himself in a sort of vision quest. In this spiritual voyage outside the body, the shaman would commonly experience a non-ordinary shift in time and space. He would visit exotic places and other times.

He would do this as a service to his tribe, for while in this trance he would typically receive the spiritual guidance necessary to lead them. In this sense, the shaman represents a viable visionary who sees all and knows all from this special vantage point. He can see into the future to plot his tribe's course to safety in the coming days and see into the past to sort out the intentions of ancestors and the guidance of spirits who had set them on the path that they now find themselves.

The vantage point that this inner work provided was better than one could find by scaling a mountaintop or climbing a tree, although the mountaintop would bring one closer to the spirits of the sky and the ancestors above us. This inner voyaging was a way of departing the ordinary world of the here and now to explore answers in the past and the future. It was a way of visiting other places, including nonphysical realms. The answers not apparent to our physical eyes and ears could be beyond our space and time but still within reach.

Often the shaman would be selected for the position based on his physical attributes. Maybe he would be lame or have a bad eye, which removed him from the hunting party but made him ideal to act as the tribe's shaman. He could not rely on his body, and this facilitated his attunement to his inner world.

Thus did the shaman develop other pertinent skills by going deep within himself in an altered state of consciousness, wherein his conscious awareness in a heightened state would become his new eyes and ears. This is something unique and outside ordinary human perception. It gave him new insight that others did not readily possess.

We do know, too, that vision quests were not limited to shamans alone—at least not in the case of North American Indians. In these cultures, young men would climb mountains or seek other special places of quiet and solitude in which to undergo their own personal vision quest. In these cases, young persons would seek personal answers about their lives and their destiny. These vision quests could last many days, a feature that was common to the samadhi mystics of India also, who performed similar vision quests.

They would not drop out of these vision quests to return to normal consciousness until they had reached the place and time they needed to visit and received the answers that had meaning for them. Only then would they return to normal consciousness. If they dropped out of the trance-like state of the vision quest before reaching their destination and attaining their needed insight, they would then focus on entering the trance-like state again.

Typically, young men of the tribe would go on such vision quests before becoming full adults and joining the other men of the tribe in hunting, which was the sacred act of becoming one with the animals with whom they interacted. These vision quests were personal quests, whereas the shaman of the tribe would enter the trance-like state for the good of the entire community, not just the individual.

In many tribes of North America these trance-like journeys into the spirit realm would be called something like dream walking or spirit walking. Different tribes described it in different ways. It is apparent that in calling it dream walking there is a parallel between the shamanic experiences of entering heightened states of consciousness and the dreamwork training of young samadhi mystics in the spiritual sciences of the East.

In both cases, the dreamer or spirit walker explores non-ordinary space-time for discovery and insight and has vivid and lucid observations of another time and place. In both traditions, too, only specially trained people entered special voyages of discovery. Not everyone was accepted as a chela-in-training to samadhi mysticism. Not everyone had the opportunity to serve as a shaman. This is special training, but something that probably anyone could learn if given the opportunity.

I recall speaking at a symposium a few years ago in Wisconsin. It was at a lake and near a former Native American burial ground There were many speakers invited from across North America, including many shamans from various tribes.

I spoke about time travel and tried to convince people there that anyone with the right intent and focus could sidestep ordinary time and space. With respect for the many shamans who graced the gathering, I noted that samadhi mystics and shamans do this all the time, and they do it much better than I could demonstrate. I then added that most of us could never become samadhi masters or shamans but could nonetheless experience time travel in our own lives.

After my presentation, a very distinguished shaman from a distant part of the country came over. He had a wide smile on his face, and he put a supporting hand on my shoulder. He told me that I had it right. This *was* something that a nonnative who was not a shaman could experience on a personal level. So often nonnatives try to interpret native traditions that he thought it was good to hear something closer to the truth, like what I had said about their tradition of spirit walking being a universal experience that anyone could explore.

To replicate their spiritual journeys, one would need a concentrated level of focus and intent and a willingness to enter a heightened state of consciousness. If willing and properly trained, however, anyone is capable of learning the techniques needed to embark on a spiritual vision quest.

In the coming chapter, we will examine some practical exercises that you can employ to sample the rarified air of this sort of heightened consciousness for discovery and insight in non-ordinary space-time. The pathless land begins with one step in another direction, but nobody can take that step for you. It will likely lead you beyond ordinary time and space and beyond the limited view of reality that most people perceive. We see so little in our physical world with our eyes and limited understanding of reality. There is so much more beyond this physical world of normal time and space that could be explored.

THIRTEEN

Common Misconceptions about Time

We will now explore how people can freely move along the timeline to experience actual shifts in time. So, let us be truly clear about what time really is and what time is not. Time, as we commonly conceive of it culturally, is an illusion. We find it comfortable and reassuring that we feel able to measure time accurately and even attempt to use these measurements to make predictions and arrange our lives. Again, however, I will attempt to convince you that this sense of time is an illusion.

Certainly, we find it convenient to have a common framework of what time is so that we can agree upon a common meeting time, set goals with target dates, and catch planes and buses on a predictable schedule. Life would be chaotic in a modern society without some agreement on scheduling. And we love to talk about a car that can reach sixty miles per hour in four seconds or an athlete who can run one mile in four minutes or less. We relish that we can beat the clock, and we go to great lengths to do so.

We keep close tabs on what we consider the passing of time with wristwatches, wall clocks, stopwatches, and even atomic timepieces. I wonder who will keep the time when we are gone, and if anyone left behind will even really care.

Nonetheless, we seem to gain confidence and comfort as a species by our ability to measure things. We can only begin to imagine anything outside the three dimensions of the boxes in which we live with sides, top and bottom, and some vague sense of depth "out there," in our feeble attempt to grapple with expanding space.

But this is not easy for us. We tend to think always in linear terms, and time is no exception. We think of a starting point, a midpoint, and an end point somewhere in the horizon ahead of us. Somehow, we like to think of our life's journey coming to an end point. Maybe that gives us a sense of completion or progress in reaching an end to our journey. But what if our journey never ends and the road continues without end?

Our ancestors were quite convinced that they would fall off the edge of the world if they moved too far in any one direction. Apparently, it never occurred to them in their linear thinking that the world's horizon could curve back on itself. This would enable you to walk in one direction and eventually circle the world and find yourself back in the same place you had begun.

This is likely how it works with time. Time is not linear and finite but endless and everlasting, and as such, it loops back on itself. It might help to think of time as a conveyor belt that loops around and around. It is like getting on the Circle route bus in London and riding for miles and miles all day long, yet continually returning to your point of origination.

We just happen to be standing physically on one point we have chosen to experience one version of reality. Our physical perception is focused on this point in time. Most likely, other versions of us live everywhere on the time loop, just as the individual on a circular route bus actualizes his presence everywhere on the bus line as he changes his relative position and perspective. We can project intellectually to consider ourselves somewhere in the past or future but must wait for our bus to take us there.

A test of this theory is for you to meditate and visit yourself in the past or the future in a lucid, conscious dream. If the appearance and actions of the person you observe do not fit some previous perception of yourself, then it represents some other version of yourself that is not stored in your memory nor reflected in your current self-image.

We identify with the instant that we can perceive where we are situated physically within our frame of reference. But you might consider, as some modern physicists have, that every conscious thought that we have launched with mental and emotional energy has created mirror doubles of ourselves. This ability to manifest thought potentially creates other aspects of ourselves that can live elsewhere on the continuous timeline as we project our thoughts at the speed of light beyond the limitations of normal space-time. People who reportedly travel in time to their past or their future, as done routinely by shamans and samadhi mystics, observe their earlier or later selves elsewhere along the looped timeline while appearing side by side in a conscious energy body.

Einstein's theory of special relativity in considering time as a component of our lives saw the relative impact of the observer in how a person perceives time. There are several instants that we might realistically call "now," as light crosses the "now plane" of everyone in a different instant, depending on one's relative location. As a human being, I seem able to only focus personal perception on the situation in front of me where light is crossing my "now plane" in the instant that I am observing.

As we experience it in the mundane reality that we perceive, this law of physics is a limitation of the physical world. But cutting-edge physicists today are beginning to theorize about the realistic possibility of alternate realities and alternate universes outside our frame of reference and within the grander total scope of a multiverse. These alternate realms could be just beyond our grasp and beyond the scope of our restricted view from our boxed-in experience of a three-dimensional material world. Getting beyond the boxes that restrict our vision would seem to be beyond our abilities as physical three-dimensional beings with only a view of things on the right, the left, and vertically within these boxes.

Let us again consider philosopher P. D. Ouspensky's suggestion that the only way to see outside our boxed-in existence as three-dimensional beings is to escape our limitation through meditation into a state of higher consciousness. The walls, floor, and ceiling of our confined area might appear to be real obstructions but could also be self-imposed restrictions. Based on our understanding of reality, we accept boundaries that we feel we cannot push. These imposed restrictions are readily accepted by our brain, our mind, and our lower consciousness.

But our *heightened* consciousness, associated with our higher self or essential life spirit, is not limited physically. It feels free to extend beyond our material bodies. Consequently, the ability of shamans and Eastern mystics to experience time shifts seems appropriate. People who describe personal time shifts that appear to happen randomly seem to enter into them in an altered state of consciousness. That enables them to sidestep what we consider ordinary reality and normal time.

Light, according to Professor Einstein, seems to play a key role in determining time. In addition to the role of time in initializing and actualizing life by crossing a "now plane," light becomes the speed limit of the physical universe. Traveling at the speed of light, Einstein suggests, would enable a person to exceed the barrier of time. To go back in time, therefore, one would need to travel at the speed of a billion miles per second. Apparently, that's the speed of time travel. He cautioned, however, that a physical body that travels the speed of light would turn into pure energy.

Note how he specifies that such a speed limit restricts material matter. But consciousness can travel outside the physical body at a speed as rapid as light energy itself. In fact, consciousness would appear to travel at the speed of light. After all, consciousness is light and light is consciousness, according to the tenets of tantric yoga. Yoga considers the role of light and consciousness as the divine combination of Shakti and Shiva in absolute Creation. In this philosophy, again, light is always filled with consciousness, and consciousness is always filled with light—from the source of all Creation down to the smallest aspect of our physical existence.

Timelessness of Spirits Who
Contact Us

Outside of the physical realm with its restrictive laws of physics, the spirit realm enjoys a freedom beyond what we experience in normal time and space. This is the difference between the manifest world of matter, which appears to be frozen, and the world of unmanifest energy, which is seemingly fluid as Spirit.

Consider the spirit realm. Outside spirits who contact us do not appear bound by time as we experience it. They do not absorb, transform, or project light. Light does not reflect upon them. They are not light beings in the same sense we are.

Ghosts live out their past lives as though time is no barrier to them. Often, we experience ghosts, both human and animal, who re-create a time outside of ours.

As a former ghost hunter, I have witnessed deceased people acting out scenes from the past before my very eyes. It is like walking into another time, without leaving the site. I have seen settlers, wagon trains, and farmers as phantom images in old period costumes. To stumble on such a site is like sidestepping into the past while remaining in the same place. The place is the same, but everything looks different, as though you are seeing it through the veils of time as it once appeared.

Surely other spirits live outside our time restrictions as well. Angels and nature spirits as nonphysical beings are not bound by physical restrictions as we are and can move freely at the speed of light beyond any of the time barriers we seem to experience.

Energy can move at the speed of light and ignore the speed limits that we seem to experience in terms of time barriers.

Thoughtforms and anything created by our manifested thoughtforms can move at the speed of light outside any time barrier. That would be true of the thoughtforms of all conscious life-forms. Manifest energy in the form of human beings, when properly focused as heightened, conscious energy, can travel outside our mundane, physical time barriers.

When we consider the range of "now" instants that can exist on a looped timeline, then we must consider time as limitless. We must begin to think of timelessness as the point at which time truly loses meaning, as we view it now. Purely as a convenience of measurement, then, we set arbitrary points along the timeline for appointments and consider each instant as either "sooner" or "later," as rational mathematician Gottfried Leibniz suggested. Leibniz once postulated that there is a dichotomy with our world of Creation below and God above us in a spirit realm he called the grand creation, the realm of God and unmanifest energy. The lower physical world, where we live our mundane lives, is the realm of manifest energy.

The Practicality of Living in the Moment

Of course, where we stand in the light of day at a specific instant known as our "now" grounds us and seems to give us traction that is practical. Living in the moment helps us to focus our physical being on a specific time and place. For the analytical brain, or lower mind, it is more helpful to focus on the present, where we can apply our physical powers. That is where you can put your feet firmly on the ground, grasp hold of tasks physically in front of you, and wrap your grip around challenges that are immediately before you.

Most people find it stressful to focus on the past or worry about the future. The present moment is where we feel most comfortable as physical beings. Should you visit the future or past as a time-traveling mystic or accidental drop-in, however, you would quickly find that your presence there is restricted to the role of observer with new eyes and new ears. As an interloper to this new time, you might find it difficult to function with normal hearing and other normal ways of perception. You are out of your place, in a very real sense. It is not the same as standing on your two feet, firmly in the here and now.

To return to our metaphor of the circular route bus line, you might consider yourself a passenger who is visiting every stop along the way. Despite this, you feel perfectly comfortable only at your home stop. That is where you get off the bus to return to your house, make coffee, and tend your garden. Everywhere else, you are a visitor. Traveling forward or backward on the timeline, you are a disembodied spirit, an energy body driven by consciousness.

From Sensory Perception to Conscious Awareness

Many personal accounts of what we commonly call time shifts or slips in time suggest that time travelers do not always hear sounds in the alternate realities they encounter. If they do, the sounds seem different or selective. What they often report is a surreal parallel reality in which the world appears different. In fact, when they try to assess what they are seeing, their sensory perception seems to fail them. They seem to witness something that looks familiar, but it's a little distorted or discolored.

This is not hard to accept if we consider that they are slipping out of time from a physical body with their five senses and entering a time slip in an alternate reality. In making that leap, as we have established, one needs to enter a state of heightened consciousness. In that state, the physical five senses that you left behind are replaced by conscious awareness. Awareness may be very keen, but it does not function exactly like your senses of sight, hearing, touch, taste, and smell do.

You may have experienced something like this shift from sensory perception to conscious awareness in some of your dreams, if those dreams were vivid and lucid. In such a dream state, things seem to appear a little different. We do not seem to move in the same way, hear in the same way, or see things as they appear to us in the physical world.

I fondly recall working with Midwest cowboy poet Bruce Vance on his revealing books *DreamScape* and *MindScape* at the Theosophical Publishing House. Vance beautifully describes the kind of perceptive awareness that a dreamer or person in a meditation might likely exhibit. Nothing is exactly the way similar things appear when one is in a waking, physical body. The raised state of consciousness that takes a person to new heights in a lucid dream or meditation carries a conscious awareness that gives an intuitive understanding of things. Light does not reflect off objects in the same manner that you have come to know and trust in your physical world as a reflection processed by your eyes. Nor does sound resonate and move in the wave patterns with which we are otherwise familiar.

Vance describes our world of lucid dreams and out-of-body meditations as a slightly different world with a slightly different hue, as we perceive it with our consciousness. He suggests that you will likely *taste* colors there and *feel* fragrances. You may have an awareness that transcends physical sensations because you have truly transcended to another level of reality.

Our Complete Energy Bodies

Your higher consciousness exists outside your body as a nonphysical energy that can travel at the speed of sound, just as the subtle energy bodies that surround your physical body have energy and properties of their own beyond the physical realm. The Hindu model of the total human being posits that spiritual bodies of energy and function surround the dense material core of our being. Together these esoteric bodies combine with the physical core body to form the complete human being.

We instinctively draw upon the energy of these subtle outer bodes to sustain and drive our life force, as these energy bodies generate our emotional energy, mental energy, intuitive energy, psychological energy, causal connection, and our spiritual body. They have many different names, including ancient Sanskrit designations.

In terms of conscious awareness, our causal body enables us to intuit, perceive, and correspond with greater things around us. On a higher level, too, we see the emotional, mental, and spiritual energy bodies that surround us in our completeness as touchstones providing us with a deeper esoteric awareness of the nature of things.

As mentioned previously, going beyond physical restrictions to the realm of Spirit requires new ears and new eyes, as prescribed in the Christian Bible. "Having eyes, see ye not and having ears, hear ye not?" Jesus Christ challenged his disciples in Mark 8:18 in the King James Version of the Bible. He rebuked them for their lack of spiritual discernment.

All seven letters to the church in Matthew 13:9 end with the following advice: "He that hath an ear, let him hear," with reference to people who were "to know the mysteries of the kingdom of heaven" (Matthew 13:11). Revelation 3:6 refers to ears to "hear what the Spirit saith." Hebrews 4:7 advises us to learn to "hear His voice."

Great teachers and masters have long admonished their seekers to learn to listen better, hear better, and knock on open doors of understanding. Great masters generally ask more of their students than passive observation. They ask their students to reach beyond the five perceptive skills of the ordinary physical world to attain deeper insight.

You are probably thinking that everyone, based on experience, can listen carefully with their ears and see with their eyes everything important around them, to discern what is important, right? But what if there is a deeper level of perception involved here—a level beyond the five perceptive senses of our ordinary, physical experience? After all, that is where masters usually direct us to seek deeper truths.

Samadhi mystics in their out-of-body meditations do go deeper and explore with new ears and new eyes. So do shamans who sit very still and quiet for hours and even spend days in deep trances that take them on their vision quests beyond normal space-time.

Their heightened consciousness endows them with a new sense of perception and intuitive, energized awareness. With our knowledge of how they reach these altered states of awareness and our knowledge of how people effectively engage in lucid dreams that transport them outside normal space-time, we can learn to engage heightened awareness ourselves.

To reach this level of conscious awareness, one must learn to sit very still and put the physical body to sleep. One must learn to tune out external and internal distractions to find the quiet, still point within the center of our being, where Spirit resides. One must begin deep rhythmic breathing to invigorate the energy centers of the total body. One must clear the lower mind and focus on the intent to leave one's physical body. When the body is thus properly prepared, the spirit is free to leave on a voyage of discovery. Energized consciousness will take you there, and the new perceptive awareness of your subtle energy bodies will travel with you.

FOURTEEN

Traveling at the Speed of Light through All Time Barriers

To travel to another time along the timeline, as we have seen in the theory of special relativity of Nobel Prize–winner Albert Einstein, you would need to travel at the speed of light. That may sound difficult for a person to handle; however, the professor suggested that matter would turn into pure energy when traveling at this speed.

People generally think they move quickly if they can run a mile in less than four minutes. It takes most people more than five seconds to run just fifty yards. Of course, our legs don't move as quickly as those of a dog, a horse, or a cat. But we have technology at our disposal. We can hop in a fast car and accelerate to a rate of sixty miles per hour in just a few seconds.

That's nothing compared to the speed of light, the speed you would need to transcend the time barrier. According to Einstein's calculations, cosmic light travels at a relative speed of 186,355 miles per second as a rule; this is considered by many to be a universal constant. If you could travel that fast you could go around the world seven and a half times in one second. That's like going 670 million miles per hour in your car. But then you would turn into pure energy in a flash.

So, put it out of your head that you are going to ride in a time machine into the past or future. That flashy DeLorean can't take you back to the future, either. Both you and your chariot would likely burst into a glorious bright light. That is what happens when manifest energy of a material nature returns to unmanifest energy of a purely energetic nature.

But just because you can't ride into the future or walk into the past doesn't mean you can't traverse time. The past and future are neatly laid out before you like a conveyor belt. You can reach beyond our seemingly restrictive time barrier in the here and now by simply traveling at the speed of light with our energized consciousness, independent of our physical body.

As we have established, the one aspect of yourself that *can* travel at the speed of light is your consciousness, which exists outside your physical body and is pure energy itself. Energy centers known as chakras are housed in every one of your subtle energy bodies in addition to your physical body. Your energized subtle bodies are ready to move outside your physical self in exploration.

From a tantric yoga point of view, the twin alliance of Shiva and Shakti as consciousness and light universally drives and sustains all of life. In her amazing book *Light and Vibration: Consciousness, Mysticism & the Culmination of Yoga,* Swami Sivananda Radha suggests that all consciousness is infused with light, and all light is bathed in consciousness from the point of Creation outward, throughout all the cosmos to our very being. Hence, consciousness is light, an energy that projects outward at the known speed of the universe until it reaches its goal. The target when reached is infused with conscious energy and then transforms that conscious energy outward. Such energy never dies but is regenerated.

People, then, become human generators that absorb, process, and transform energy. We have an abundance of conscious energy. Most people utilize it only to a small degree, but it can be tapped for so much more.

Our conscious energy can move freely at the speed of light, separate and apart from our physical limitations. Our light body is formless, weightless, invisible, and has material substance. I am certain that you have sent voiceless thought messages beyond vast distances instantaneously or received them. Most people are somewhat aware when loved ones think of them or project thoughts about them. Many people seem to know that their phone is going to ring before it does. Others are somehow sensitive to the emotional anguish and thoughts of close relations even when they are miles apart. Isn't it amazing how quickly our thoughts can travel as pure conscious energy?

It's not just us, of course. Whales, according to researchers at the Whale Museum in Friday Harbor, Washington, have been recorded communicating across oceans, given that the vibrational waves of their energized thoughts travel huge distances in a flash.

Like shamans and Eastern mystics, you can move freely throughout space-time only if you learn to enter a state of heightened consciousness, leaving behind the confusion of the monkey mind that prevents you from reaching a quiet, still point deep within, calming the body long enough for Spirit to step outside.

Isn't it ironic in a sense that you need to still your body and become inwardly calm and tranquil to reach the speed of light on a higher plane? Simply stated, you need to get out of the way of yourself to let your higher self simply spring forward.

Beyond Linear Limits of a Three-Dimensional, Material World

J. Alfred Prufrock in T. S. Eliot's seminal poem "The Love Song of J. Alfred Prufrock" measured out his life in coffee spoons. His life was carefully measured in every way, yet he finds himself worried that time was running out, as he wastes his days on insignificant concerns about his physical appearance. He is hopeful that "there will be time" for his many unfulfilled ambitions. In search of more time for everything he wants to discover, he wastes his time walking down dark streets that lead nowhere. He is a careful man who measures his every step yet feels deeply depressed that he is simply standing in place and beginning to decay.

We are a lot like Eliot's sad man in the poem. Eliot seemed to think that Prufrock was not unusually unimaginative and stagnant but rather typical of people on the wheel of life, slowly dying in one spot.

As stated before but bears repeating here, we measure everything in our drab, unimaginative lives. It is sort of the human condition in a way. It is almost as though putting a tape measure in every room and weighing everything in our presence gives us some measure of control that enables us to transcend our physical limitations. In fact, it simply reinforces the understanding that our world has many walls and physical barriers.

But knowing where a wall begins and how long, tall, and thick it is by some exercise of measurement does not allow us to walk through the wall. Our physical world has barriers and restrictions. And every day when we measure everything around us, we convince ourselves how truly boxed in we really feel.

We have no frame of reference for anything outside our material, three-dimensional world, imagine as we might. We, too, are like Prufrock, wandering down dark alleys that lead us nowhere meaningful. In the end, we find ourselves looking into a mirror, realizing that we have grown old and come to the end of the line.

We have this linear approach to life that things always come to the end of the line, but there is also a hope for "a time to come," as Prufrock dreamed. In truth, it is our linear approach to life that measures it in limiting ways. Things never really measure up as we would hope.

Sadly, this is the only way we see things, given our blind trust in eyes that process reflected light upside down without deeper penetration. We do not upgrade to new eyes for better vision. We trust our ability to measure the accuracy of our eyes with charts, and with exercises to sharpen our eyesight.

We cannot conceive what we cannot measure. And what we cannot conceive, we do not perceive. So, nothing outside our grasp has meaning to us. We simply do not and cannot believe what we do not see with our eyes or measure with our hands.

A Reductionist View of the Material World

Our world, then, is a contrived schematic, carefully marked in inches and feet, in ounces and pounds, and mass density that we have concocted as convenient measures to make us feel in control. Again, in the end, however, we find ourselves confined to living in 1,250 square ft. homes with 16.5 cu. ft. refrigerators, 17 ft. x 21 ft. master bedrooms, and double-car garages that can accommodate up to 22 ft. vehicles. We set our thermostats to 68 degrees in winter and our air conditioners on automatic during summer. We set the clock at 7:00 a.m. each morning to make the coffee to start our days at 8:30 a.m. after a 20-minute commute of some 4.5 miles. We park our cars in designated parking spots every day and then return home at 5:00 p.m. We get up the next day at 7:00 a.m. to start the day with two cups of coffee, our jolt to energize us. Yes, we do measure out our lives in coffee spoons.

We measure the growth of our children in inches on a wall in the kitchen. We fret when the waist size of our pants changes, contrary to our hopes and fears. We stand in front of the mirror to see how slowly our hair grows and if it's changing color or thinning. And still we hope "there will be a time" beyond this drab life of inches and clock-watching when we will explore a richer life beyond our four walls.

This is the reductionist life of materialism by which everything is measured physically. It is the manifest world of seeming inflexibility. Nothing bends but instead remains rigid. Broken bones take forever to heal. It all appears so permanent and set in stone. We dream of achieving fluidity and the ability to change and break out of the boxes that enclose us, but things move so slowly in the manifest world that this appears to be nearly immobile.

This is an illusion, of course. Our physical world, mundane as it feels to us, is nonetheless filled with manifest energy in a state of temporary suspension apart from its purely unmanifest energy. Change is free and easy, constantly in motion. In truth, creation is all about change, and change is constant. We are simply stuck here in a temporary state of manifest energy where things are energized like gelatin that is only half formed and a bit sticky—not fluid, but not solid either.

Our world is only half formed, in a sense. It is material, as measured by our physical restrictions, and pliable as energy that in its semi-slumbering state has a little flexibility and potential to change.

We are stuck in the middle of this world, part spirit and part physical. You are a human hybrid, composed partially of light and partially of physical matter. In truth, you are more than the sum of your parts. You are a complex being of almost unlimited potential. The trick, of course, is learning how to unlock this potential and step outside the box.

FIFTEEN

Moving in the Light

It might seem difficult if not impossible for us as human beings to live beyond the linear limits of our three-dimensional world. That is certainly the cultural attitude we inherit. That orientation is further defined by our personal frame of reference. But I would suggest that that limited view is based more on our perception of walls around us and our relative situation in our environment than absolute restrictions. Our physical senses allow us to see only three dimensions and a fixed world that is set in form without any flexibility that would allow us to reach beyond what we immediately see.

Several years ago I met a sage from India who forever changed my own view on such human limitations. He was as mysterious as the message he gave me. He delivered this message over time in a series of three strange phone calls when I was working on the second floor of the Theosophical Publishing House in Wheaton, Illinois. I had no idea who this man was or why he'd singled me out for his phone calls.

I had just started working for the publishing division of the publishing house. I shared an office at the end of the second floor of the building, above the organization's Quest Bookshop and just down the hallway from my personal apartment on the second floor.

It was a sunny office space that enjoyed an amazing amount of sunlight that streamed through the wraparound windows in my half of the suite. I shared my corner of the office with a lot of happy aloe vera plants and citrus plants that soaked up the intense natural light and grew to immense size, wrapping themselves around all the windows like pretty ribbons

I hadn't been working there long before I received a most unusual phone call one summer afternoon. The call came out of the blue and left me scratching my head afterward. On the other end of my landline was the voice of what sounded like an old man from India, a gentleman with a very thick accent.

He was quite polite and invited me on a lightning tour of India in the fall. He said that he led these tours of India every year and found September to be the ideal time to go. According to him, this tour would change my life forever.

I asked him who he was and why he had selected me to invite on his tour. He ignored both questions and continued to promote the value of this journey to me personally.

It occurred to me that he was probably calling from India on the landline, yet the long-distance phone call was quite clear. It was so clear it was as if he was in the room with me.

Regretfully, I told him that I had just started my job and was far too busy to take what sounded like a long vacation trip. I had just replaced Clarence "Pete" Pederson, an elderly man who had served as publication director for many years. In addition, I was helping to launch a new national magazine, *The Quest,* and developing a syndicated radio show for thirty-seven stations as well as a companion television series for thirteen stations. I was working in our little sound studio to help produce audio and video programs to add to our book line. If that was not enough, I was organizing public seminars and visiting regional media for events at our facility and larger presentations in Chicago. I was busy at that point and could not consider any personal trips.

The Indian gentleman kindly listened to everything I said and then repeated that I should join him on his lightning tour for an enlightening experience that would change my life.

It occurred to me that he must have dialed my office in an attempt to reach my predecessor, Pete Pederson. After all, Pete and I had the same office and same phone extension. I asked the Indian gentleman if he had meant to call Pete and not me. He insisted that he wanted to speak to me and repeated that this information was important for me personally.

After this first phone call, I wondered how he had located me. It dawned on me that he might have reached my office through the switchboard, since I was new and unknown. So, I asked our information officer, who fielded calls to the Theosophical Society in America and routed them to the appropriate phone extension throughout our two buildings. She just stared at me blankly and replied she would have remembered routing a call by an elderly man with a thick Indian accent. She assured me that he had dialed me directly.

So, I began to think that the whole phone call was some elaborate prank being played on me by someone at our building or the administration building across the street. To reveal the person possibly behind such a prank, I described my phone call to various people on staff who I thought might have been able to disguise their voice enough to sound like an elderly man with a thick Indian accent.

All of the people I confronted face-to-face, however, just stared at me without blinking, smiling, or displaying any other sort of telltale sign that an exposed gagster might reveal under such close scrutiny.

I received another phone call from my mystery caller several days later. Again he urged me to join him on his lightning tour of India in the fall and gave the same reasons for my participation. I quizzed him about his name and affiliation once more and asked him why he had selected me. Again he refused to answer these questions. He only said that he had chosen me as a person who would greatly benefit from the tour.

After giving him my reasons why I couldn't go on his tour that autumn and once again hearing his promise of a life-changing experience ahead of me, we ended our second call cordially. He said that he would call me again after I had taken some time to reflect on his offer.

This mystery man with the Indian accent was beginning to stir my curiosity. I still had no clue as to his identity, location, or connection to me, however. He didn't seem to know me and yet he insisted that he had singled me out. I was so new at the Theosophical Publishing House that it seemed unlikely that anyone outside my friends, family, and coworkers at our two buildings really knew I was there at all.

But I had asked everyone I could think of about the man and his strange phone calls, without learning anything about him. Nobody in our two buildings had ever heard about an elderly Indian gentleman who led annual lightning tours to India, although many people seemed to think that it was indeed a chance of a lifetime.

It occurred to me that the Theosophical Society as an international organization with headquarters in India probably had a number of members from India. So, I called the international headquarters in Adyar to learn anything they might know about such a man. But that proved to be a dead end, too, as nobody there was able to help me whatsoever.

Unable to sort out this puzzle, I tried to put this man and his curious phone calls out of my mind and forget that he had ever called me. Days rolled by without another call, so I began to forget about my mystery caller altogether.

Then one late summer afternoon, the phone at my corner office rang abruptly. I must say that I had a funny feeling immediately, as though I recognized the way the phone rang and knew it would be an unusual call.

The same elderly gentleman with the Indian accent asked whether I had thought about his offer and reconsidered. He reminded me that it would be a life-changing experience and a unique opportunity for me.

Again I was amazed how clear his voice seemed on this long-distance call. I assumed that he was calling from India but really had no idea where he was located. Most phone calls, even local calls on that landline, were not that clear.

I disappointed him again with a negative response to his offer, while trying to sound most appreciative and polite. Clearly, this old man thought that he was offering me a special opportunity and trying to get me to join him on his tour, despite my narrow, measured view of things.

Realizing that he had failed to recruit me after numerous personal invitations, he then changed tactics. He said he could offer me something else that would change my life forever. He said that I did not need to leave my home or my job. He advised me how to meditate in the light, something he said would have far-reaching benefits if done correctly. He explained that this was an incredibly special form of yoga. I asked him what kind of light was needed and how I should meditate.

He explained that I should meditate in the early morning light beside running water. He said that the first light of day held special properties. I responded that we had a pond on the office grounds next to a huge tree. I told him that I could place a blanket on the grass under the tree and meditate beside the pond in the early morning light. There was only a little recirculating pump that stirred the water for a fountain, and it provided a tiny spray of water. That fountain and the fish in the pond were the only things that broke the stillness of the pond.

He said little about the pond as I described it, only that it was a start. He said that it was important that I begin to practice this morning meditation regularly. "You sit in the light, meditate in the light, and move in the light," he told me. "Be in the light."

I asked him what he meant by "move" in the light. He responded that I must live in the light and become one with the light. I wondered aloud whether meditating in the light would train me to move in the light and become one with the light in time. As I recall, he said that I could only accomplish any of that with meditation.

That was the last time I spoke with this mysterious sage. I subsequently found a blanket and placed it under the large cypress tree next to the pond. There I began to meditate in the early morning sunlight.

I could feel the difference immediately, as the warmth of the sun and gurgling sound of the pond had a profound effect upon me. It was more than the warm feeling of the sun or the sound of the water. I felt transported to a new level of consciousness.

I understood, once I began these morning meditations, that altering my consciousness and putting myself in the light would indeed transport me. I found myself leaving my body and having profound out-of-body experiences during these meditation sessions.

But who was this man with this sage advice? I assumed that I would never know but then decided to try looking for clues in our own bookshop. I asked our bookstore manager where the most reliable books by Indian mystics were situated among all of the books we carried on yoga and meditation.

She responded that "the good stuff" from respected Eastern teachers was located in one corner of the shop and pointed me in the right direction. I wandered into a corner and immediately saw one book that seemed to call out to me. It was displayed face-out on a table easel.

I turned it over and started reading the back cover. The book was written by an Indian master on his approach to meditating beside running water in the early morning sunlight. It said that he was also famous for organizing lightning tours to India every year in the fall. At the bottom, it listed when he was born and the year he died. This man had died a couple of years earlier.

That made me think that the phone calls I had received from my mystery man were indeed long-distance calls. It appeared to me that this master had called me from the great beyond. Clearly, he had learned to move in the light, for it appeared that death, distance, and time were no restrictions to him. He was indeed a master.

But why had he singled me out? A few years later when I moved from Illinois to Minnesota to work for another publisher, I seemed to get my answer. Or at least I found a special use for his training, other than personal meditation.

My new roommate in Saint Paul was a young woman who developed brain cancer that couldn't be removed by surgery or painful chemotherapy. When we placed her in hospice care to spend her last days confined to a bed she would never leave, it occurred to me that my thirty-two-year-old friend might benefit from meditating in the light. So, we began to practice the Indian mystic's meditation technique together.

It's funny how the idea came to me and how I remembered the Indian master's technique in the middle of my friend's sad hospitalization. I saw how forlorn she was to be bedridden with no prospect of ever walking out of that room or going anywhere ever again. It seemed that time had run out on her.

My dying friend loved *Star Trek* and how the crew of the science-fiction television show could relocate by stepping into a transporter device that illuminated them and moved their atoms across space to rematerialize far away.

So, I asked her if she would like to try a little meditation exercise that could move her in the light just like the *Star Trek* crew and their transporter. She had been depressed and unable to speak but quickly nodded yes to my suggestion, smiling with anticipation.

I told her that if we did these exercises perfectly, she could leave the confines of that room and leave her pain behind without her ever having to step out of bed. We moved her a little closer to the sunlight that streamed through a window. There was a huge water fountain just outside the hospice doors, one donated by friends of hospice patients. In the weeks that followed, I guided my dying friend daily on an out-of-body journey that brought her a great sense of release and freedom.

Together we seemed to move in the light through various planes of reality, hand in hand. In each new level of reality, the light seemed to change in intensity and color from white to red, orange, yellow, green, and eventually blue.

She seemed to greatly enjoy these voyages as we meditated in the light together. She seemed to find it easier to do so each day, and in time she appeared comfortable making her way in the light on her own. When I commented how comfortable she had become with these meditations and asked whether she felt that she could now move freely in the light by herself, she said the first word she'd been able to utter in weeks.

"Yes!" she said positively, with a smile. She tried to squeeze my hand as though to accent her enthusiasm.

I told the head nurse that my friend was comfortable with her situation now and was ready to move on. The next day, my former roommate was declared legally dead. She had physically died, but I knew that she would be alive and just fine. Like the Indian mystic, death would not confine her, and neither would physical limitations.

It dawned on me that a change in consciousness was key to her new freedom. She was no longer tied to one place and one time but instead could move in a conscious body to various alternate realities, carried at the speed of light by the glow of the sun.

After she died, my roommate's bedroom, emptied weeks earlier of all furniture and fixtures, played music from a corner where a stereo once sat. Pink ribbons once tucked away in secret spots for a Christmas never celebrated appeared in places where my roommate's cat would find them for play. When I visited the cemetery to visit her grave, I heard her voice inside my head, telling me very clearly, *you will not find me here.*

I think it's profound how that old man with the thick Indian accent had singled me out years earlier and insisted that I learn to meditate in the light. He was right that it would change my life forever. Had he also foreseen how I would later have the opportunity to share this information with my friend in ways that would impact *her* life forever?

It occurred to me how many more people could benefit from this information. After all, there is an infinite amount of light to share.

SIXTEEN

Our Physical World Is Energized and Conscious

Like me, most of your life you have probably felt that change comes slowly, if at all, in our physical world, for we live in the manifest world of matter. It's a material world of solid objects. It hardly seems like a fluid realm filled with a lot of flexibility.

Our physical barriers define our world for us in many ways. When you live next to a mountain, it doesn't seem to change significantly during your lifetime. The rocks don't seem to change and certainly don't seem to move, barring something like infrequent volcanic action or earthquakes. Tectonic plates buried deep in the Earth take eons to grind against each other with enough friction to shake the planet.

I used to find this pace frustrating in my youth when I felt trapped in a world of manifest energy. Nothing seemed alive and nothing seemed to change. But that viewpoint, I later realized, was very shortsighted and incorrect.

Many trees in your life were fully grown in your youth and will probably outlive you. Endless generations of birds and squirrels live in those seemingly ageless trees. I recall breaking a bone and waiting for what seemed an eternity for natural regeneration to fuse it back together. We experience change in a very slow fashion whenever we break a bone and wait with bated breath for change that, whenever our physical bodies become injured or diseased, seems to take forever.

And so it seems to us, with our limited perceptual skills as linear, three-dimensional beings. This puts the material world of manifest energy in stark contrast with the realm of unmanifest energy, where change is quick and constant in a continuous flow.

But when I tell you that the manifest world of matter that you call our physical world is actually not as inflexible or permanent in form as it appears, I believe I have both modern science and respected metaphysics on my side.

Let us start with how physicists commonly view the stable nature of our physical world. It is often said by those who are familiar with quantum mechanics and particle theory that a chair is not as solid as it appears, and a table is not as stable as it seems.

Most of us today have come to accept that within the atomic composition of physical matter, electrons are in motion. In every atom of material matter electrons and protons are orbiting a central nucleus. The small electrically charged particles are arranged to assume a specific form. But again, the electrically charged particles are in a constant state of motion and there is a duality in this atomic structure. It is correct to think of electrons as both particles and waves in motion. They can be deemed to be energetically charged particles that also exhibit wave actions as vibrational ripples or pulses. Thus, we should keep in mind the energetic nature that underlies seemingly tranquil, stable matter in our physical world.

The scientific mysticism of the East also posits that the physical matter of our world is not completely solid or still. *The Secret Doctrine* by H. P. Blavatsky, based on stanzas from the ancient, mystical *Book of Dzyan,* summarizes the nature of Creation in fundamental propositions that form the introductory thesis for the doctrine. Significant to our discussion here, this text describes the nature of our physical world of material form as somewhat *plastic* or pliable and not completely stable or static.

The text refers to an ancient Sanskrit word by a unique spelling—*Svabhavat*—and describes it as the highest aspect of universal spirit and a "plastic essence" that fills the universe and becomes the root of all things material. This mysterious aspect of Spirit as energy both drives and sustains all life—from mere atoms to the cosmos. Furthermore, the Eastern interpretation of Svabhavat is that it is a plastic substance, a decidedly vague and inadequate definition of a deep, universal mystery into the nature of reality.

Buddhists sometimes refer to Svabhavat as a concrete aspect of the abstraction that Hindus call *Mulaprakrit,* which is the body of the soul. According to these ancient views from the East, Svabhavat and Mulaprakrit are thus considered the stuff behind the essential being of all substance and the underlying spirit behind matter. Thus, if we consider Spirit as light or energy, then these ancient spiritual texts agree with modern physics that energy is within all physical matter. We might consider the energy that underlies the physical matter of our world, then, as latent energy inherent in material form.

After weighing the concept of intelligent design or the Hindu views of light and vibration as consciousness, it would not be a stretch to assume that all physical life is infused with energetic consciousness.

If you are like me and find science challenging, perhaps you find it difficult to visualize the fluid nature of our physical world—with matter in motion and the inherent wave action of particles. To best conjure this, it always helps me to think of a gelatin mold in my refrigerator, wherein the gelatin is trying to achieve some solidity after I have poured it into a tray. After some time it assumes the appearance of being solid and firm. But upon removing it from the refrigerator I quickly learn that it has a little wiggle to it. It sways almost like a little wave upon the sea. It's not really stable, firm, or static after all.

Our physical world is indeed a little like the gelatin in the tray. It is not static and hardly lifeless. If you roll the bowl of gelatin from side to side, you will see that it is alive with energetic potential. It is spirited.

The actual energy that underlies physical matter is transcendent beyond form and function; it is everlasting. Trees appear to die, but seeds continue their life. Leaves die but become compost to continue the cycle of life. Houseplants live their lives indoors and are mostly in the shade and yet send out runners to find nearby sunlight. They seem to consciously know how to find the light and live in the light. That sounds like a sort of consciousness to me and reveals an understanding of the role of light in our world.

Nature shows us the energy behind all physical life and how it continues. We tend to think of life cycles, but really, it is just one cycle with many transitions along the way.

Nothing brought this to my attention more than the experiences I had in college building sets for theatrical productions. These sets looked realistic but were ridiculous when you examined them closely. I attempted to build something that looked like trees and roads as part of an actual landscape setting. Admittedly, I was not much good at building fake landscapes. My props would easily fall apart, so I received supplemental help from our assistant theater director. This man did everything from building floors to screwing down chairs for the audience. When he finished helping me, my set for *Our Town* almost resembled a real town.

But it was a lifeless representation and as such required a great imagination to visualize it as a real setting. There was no energy in anything we built. There was no life. At the end of every performance, when we would strike the set and put things away until the next performance, our phony representation of a town felt odd to the touch.

I believe every reader of this book knows what I'm talking about and can sense this difference, too. A plastic Christmas tree or synthetic yule wreath doesn't feel as energized and conscious as a real tree or a wreath. You can tell the difference immediately because there is no spiritual connection with consciousness. Such representations might appear similar to the real thing at first glance, but you can sense the lifelessness as soon as you come within close proximity and certainly when you handle them. You cannot connect to them on a spirit-to-spirit level.

Our physical world and the life-forms we know as real trees and rivers are electric as we experience them. They are alive with energy and consciousness. And as such, we form real bonds of connectedness with them. We might say that our physical world is pregnant with potential, as the seeds of change are hidden in everything as conscious energy, latent but in constant motion. There is no such thing as dead matter, static matter, or lifeless matter. Every aspect of physical life is alive and interrelated.

Thus, if we consider that our material world of manifest energy is not completely stable, static, and solid, even though it may appear so to our eyes, then perhaps we need to review the world that we occupy with new eyes.

What we know for sure is that change is an absolute certainty. We can be certain of the fluidity that makes this living world much more than a lifeless stage of props where actors negotiate in a makeshift reality. The ground certainly does move under our feet from time to time; and waves do carry us to distant shores. We are not stuck in a lifeless world without movement and change.

So maybe we should seriously reconsider our views on absolute reality. Maybe we are in a state of transition, sort of floating on an iceberg and moving gently with the motion of subtle waves. Maybe this physical world is not the be-all and end-all that we like to think it is. Maybe it's simply somewhere between now and another now that's just as real but not yet fully realized.

Maybe the song that sang our world into creation is still a symphony in progress, as the music of the spheres radiates down from the heavens as a divine gift that is ever unfolding and promising.

With every radiation of electromagnetic energy that infuses our lives with light comes an evolving consciousness. Ancients often considered this the mother-father principle behind Creation in progress.

With heightened consciousness we are able to see beyond the physical illusion that our world is changeless and static, and we can hear beyond the normal range of hearing that comes with our basic physical senses. In a state of heightened consciousness, maybe we can see beyond the veil and between the cracks in the worlds.

As we are interrelated and interdependent in our physical environment, we form one living system of conscious and evolving life. The
beauty of creation in nature is probably not complete without our participation, adding our light to its light and our consciousness to its consciousness in a building process that is continually evolving.

If we are truly in a condition of becoming and unfolding with new
realization as a part of this grand design, then we are always opening
new doors and entering new levels of Creation. Our consciousness
opens the door. Our light is the key.

Most accounts of time shifts suggest that people seem to experience
an altered state of consciousness beforehand. They clear their minds
and become very still and then suddenly find themselves viewing things
before them with a new perception. There is a recognizable pattern of
this in the anecdotal evidence.

This is also compatible with the approach of shamanic spirit
walkers and samadhi mystics who routinely enter deep, meditative states
of altered consciousness and report experiences outside of normal time
and space. This would appear, then, to be a reliable model.

If the purpose of our lives is to experience growth and expand
awareness, I would suggest that broadening our experiences and raising
our consciousness might fulfill our human potential to become more
aware and one with all of Creation. In reaching this level of conscious
awareness, we will likely find ourselves with new eyes and new ears to
behold more than we see on the flat surface of life.

SEVENTEEN

Some Practical Personal Exercises

This chapter will introduce you to some practical exercises to allow you to experience time shifts in a heightened state of consciousness on a personal level. Once you have sidestepped into non-ordinary reality and experienced a new time and place in this way, the likelihood of time travel will become more meaningful to you.

The exercises can take you to the past in your own vision quests to examine your life from a better perspective. They also can take you into the future to study what awaits you and to visit those dear to you. They can even allow you to speak with your ancestors. These exercises are meant to be very personal journeys of discovery to influence your life. Once you try them, you will readily see other possibilities to slightly alter the exercises for a different perspective. The exercises are flexible to better suit your needs and interests.

To some people, these exercises might look like meditation or even lucid dreaming. To others, they might look like a trance or self-hypnosis. It is easy to get lost in words, so maybe we should just think of these exercises as personal journeys of self-exploration.

Our first destination is my favorite setting and the place I love to send people. Once you add your own personal touches, this could be your favorite go-to place, as well.

➥ **Exercise: Reaching Your Ideal Healing Place**

What's Needed

- a quiet, secluded place for you to meditate
- a pad, blanket, or towel to place on the floor beneath you; an option would be a straight-backed chair
- loose-fitting, comfortable clothes
- shoes, jewelry, and any external items removed from your body

Procedure

Recline on your back with both arms and both legs outstretched to 45-degree angles. Reclining on your back is ideal, but you could also choose to sit in the chair with upright posture and your feet firmly planted on the ground.

Consciously put your physical body to sleep, beginning with your feet and focusing your attention on your body up to the top of your head. Give your physical self the permission to rest while you access your heightened consciousness.

Begin rhythmic, deep breathing and continue it through all phases of the exercise.

Focus on the energy centers of your whole body inside and outside your physical self, activating the energy of your chakra centers from your spine to the top of your head. Visualize the red energy of your root chakra, the orange energy of your causal body, the yellow energy of your mental body, the green energy of your heart center, the blue energy of your throat area, the indigo energy of your forehead, and the violet energy above your crown chakra. Collect your energy. Bring it with you on your journey. With it comes the wholeness of all your subtle energy bodies. Your heightened consciousness lives on all of these levels and can travel beyond your physical body.

Tune out all external and internal distractions until you reach a still point deep inside you and see a blank slate in your mind's eye.

Begin to paint or draw a picture of what you would consider your idea healing place, a secluded and rustic setting where you can visit whenever you need to energize yourself and recover from emotional distress, mental anguish, spiritual wounds, or physical problems.

This might be an idealized place or an actual location that is familiar to you. It can be in the known world or even on another plane of existence outside this physical world. It's your special place for your personal use whenever you might need to recover from something that ails you.

Perhaps you can think of a place on a mountain, in the woods, beside the ocean, or beside a stream or a pond. It could be a meadow or a cave. You begin to form the picture on the blank slate in your mind's eye. Make this picture as detailed as you like, but do not despair if it's sketchy. It is your idealized picture and will provide you with a road map to take you there.

Now store that picture in the back of your mind and prepare yourself for the journey ahead. When you recall that picture, you will immediately follow it automatically.

Give yourself permission to leave your physical body behind in a safe and restful position while you are gone. Now recall your picture of the special healing place and let your consciousness take you there. When you reach it, take notice of everything around you. Convince yourself that you are present there and an integral part of the place. Look at your hands. Make any changes that you feel would improve the place to make it completely comfortable and therapeutic for you.

Bask in the healing properties of where you are, knowing that it is especially designed for you to heal and rejuvenate whenever you need it. When you feel completely comfortable there, project the red, orange, yellow, green, blue, indigo, and violet energy that you have brought with you as part of your subtle energy bodies. Do not hold back.

Bask in the rejuvenating properties of your energized healing place. When you feel that you have set it up exactly the way you want it and have felt its magic, simply project your conscious attention back to your physical body.

You should find yourself immediately back in your body. Remember the picture you have created and the magic of your personal healing place. You can return there whenever you need to.

⟶Exercise: Visiting Your Parents
What's Needed

- a quiet, secluded place for you to meditate
- a straight-backed chair (or mat on which to recline on your back)
- loose-fitting, comfortable clothing with shoes, jewelry, and any external items removed

Procedure

Sit erect in your chair with feet firmly planted to ground yourself (or recline in the classic yoga "dead man pose" on your back with arms and legs extended). Do not cross anything and allow energy to flow freely within you.

Begin deep, rhythmic breathing and continue it.

Focus your attention on your body starting at your feet and working up to your head and order your physical body to become numb.

Tune out all external and internal distractions until you reach a still point deep within you. Begin to focus on the blank slate in front of your mind's eye.

On this blank slate, draw or paint a picture of one of your parents long ago when this parent first conceived of you and had first thoughts about you. The face might indicate dreams, aspirations, ambitions, and concerns about you. You can picture one of your parents in this exercise and then do the exercise again, picturing your other parent.

If you picture your parent when you were very little or just born, that is the time when you will visit. If you picture your parent before you were born or even conceived in the womb, then you will visit your parent at this specific point in time. Remember, all time is a series of "now" instants on one long, continuous time loop that is never-ending. You will now be focusing your conscious awareness on this particular instant on the timeline and experience that instant as your immediate now.

Once again, don't fret if your picture is sketchy. It should be just a sketch to guide you. You will be able to follow this picture like a perfect map to the scene you have envisioned. This is your personal vision quest.

Once the picture is formed, give yourself permission for your energy body to leave your physical location there in your meditation space and go directly to the person and time in the location you have envisioned.

When you arrive there, satisfy yourself that you are truly there by studying the details of the setting, the colors you see with your new eyes, and observe your own presence in that time and place. You will probably not be observed, as you are traveling in a nonphysical body. But your own powers of observations with heightened awareness will be keen.

Study your parent and tap in to your parent's thoughts. Project your own thought about yourself as a child and let your parent respond to this thoughtform as a stimulus.

Try to understand and relate to your parent. Gather as much insight as you can. When you feel you have learned something of personal value to you, return your focused attention to your physical body. You will instantly return to your mediation room.

⟾ **Exercise: Visiting Your Former Teachers**
What's Needed
- straight-backed chair or mat for meditation
- quiet, secluded space for your meditation
- comfortable, loose-fitting clothing with shoes and jewelry removed

Procedure
We can visit our teachers and mentors as well as our ancestors. Time and space are no barriers. They might be deceased, but you can

go back in time to visit them for insight. Perhaps you want to know something they didn't tell you. Or maybe you want a clarification. Maybe you want to realize what they really expected from you or wanted you to pursue. In the same sense, you may want to know their concerns. Wouldn't it be great to hear from them again? And wouldn't their information make more sense to you now, since you are older and perhaps more able to sort out their words?

Simply enter a state of deep meditation by grounding yourself, putting your physical body to rest, establishing a pattern of deep breathing, tuning out all external and internal distractions, and reaching a still point deep within yourself.

Assemble the energy of your subtle energy bodies to take with you, making certain that you collect everything at your disposal from the colors red, orange, yellow, green, blue, indigo, and violet, each energetic color with its own properties that correspond to your subtle energy bodies and the corresponding planes of existence. Consciousness resides on each of these subtle bodies, energized and ready for use. Make certain that you collect all of it when you leave your physical body behind.

See a blank slate in your mind's eye and focus your attention on crafting a picture of the teacher, mentor, or guide whom you want to contact. Picture them in a place you'd like to see them and at a time that you'd like to visit. There are no barriers.

Once you have sketched a rough picture of where and when you want to go and who you want to see, use this picture as a perfect map to take you beyond the room where your body reclines in perfect safety and repose. Allow yourself to leave your body and follow the blueprint you have constructed to direct you to your destination, across time and space. Remember, your consciousness exists outside the physical realm and is not restricted.

When you arrive at your destination, you might be startled to see your former mentor at this early stage. Convince yourself that you are indeed at that setting by studying the details of the setting, the colors around you, and your own presence there in an energy body.

Your mentor will not recognize you, as you are not in a physical body, but you can project a thought to your old friend, thereby triggering that person's thoughts. The thought can be a simple image of you. Picture images are strong thoughtforms. Or you could send a greeting. You need to relate this triggering thought in a way this person will comprehend, perhaps an image of an earlier you that is known to this person.

Then you can study this person and read their thoughts of you. You do not need words. In your heightened state of awareness, you have new ears and can read thoughts if you are focused.

When you sense you have learned something of value from your old teacher or mentor, you can return your focus to your reclining physical body. Then you will instantly return your consciousness and energy bodies to the room where you are meditating.

⏵ Exercise: Visit Yourself in a Previous Life

What's Needed

- a quiet, secluded place to meditate
- comfortable, loose-fitting clothing with shoes, jewelry, and any other external items removed
- a mat or blanket on which to recline on your back (or straight-backed chair if you are not comfortable reclining on your back)

Procedure

Recline on your back on the mat with arms and legs outstretched and no part of you crossed, so that energy flows freely through you. (If you opt to sit in a chair, then sit with erect posture with your feet firmly planted to ground you.)

Consciously put your physical body to sleep, beginning with your feet and focusing your attention on every part of your physical body up to your head. When the thoughts of your physical brain and lower mind have ceased to operate, then the heightened consciousness of your higher mind will begin to operate at an accelerated pace.

Focus on your energy centers on your subtle energy bodies beginning with your base chakra and its red energy and working your way up to the crown chakra and its violet energy, collecting the red, orange, yellow, green, blue, indigo, and violet energy of your total being to take with you on the journey ahead.

Begin deep, rhythmic breathing and continue this pattern.

Tune out all external and internal distractions until you reach a still point deep within your being and see a blank slate in front of your mind's eye.

On this blank slate, begin to create a picture of yourself at an earlier time, in a place you once knew. Go deeper and deeper into your core self until you go beyond the birth of your childhood to the life you lived before this lifetime. Patiently wait until the picture begins to form for you.

If this seems impossible for you after patiently waiting for the past to appear to you, then you could simply opt to form a picture of yourself at a younger age in your immediate lifetime. This can have value, too, but is not what we are primarily after here. The psychologist can put you on a couch and make you remember a time when you were small to confront your problems and gain insight into them today. But we are attempting to prove to you that you can go back in time before your birth as a child to visit yourself in an earlier incarnation. Time is no barrier for your consciousness, as it is not restricted by the laws of physics of our physical world. It operates outside physical dimensions and limitations.

Realistically, it might require great patience to form the picture of you in an earlier lifetime in the setting you once occupied in that life. But if you persist, you should be able to form a picture on the screen before your mind's eye. The picture should form itself, as you watch, as you reach deep within your eternal consciousness and recall.

When the picture is formed, even though sketchy, trust that you will relate to it as a perfect road map that can take you to this person and place beyond the time and space you now occupy. Then allow yourself the freedom to leave your physical body behind and visit that place and time.

It might take you a little longer to reach this destination, and, when you do, you might find it difficult to orient yourself at first. This is because you have no ready frame of reference to this earlier time and place. Just trust the process and allow yourself to meet the person of your past. This person is the missing link to your origins and the person you know so well.

Observe this person with the intuitive skills of your causal body, the comprehension of your mental body, the empathy of your emotional body, and the awareness of your other subtle bodies and the conscious energy they have brought for you.

If you feel that this earlier version of yourself requires an energy boost for health, inspiration, or understanding, then feel free to project the subtle body energy that you have brought with you. Maybe this person lacks spiritual or emotional energy that you can provide. This is not interfering with the karma of this person or their free will for self-determination. This is you and your life, after all. You have a natural karmic connection to this person. And you live on the same timeline, although you ordinarily perceive it at a different point along it based on your immediate orientation.

When you have learned something of this person that you feel is insightful and meaningful, return to your physical body back in the meditation room. All you need to do is shift your conscious focus back to this person reclining in the room to instantly return to your physical body.

When you have returned, you should reflect very quietly on what you have observed before restoring full sensation to your physical body, opening your eyes, and slowly rising to your feet.

This is a backward glance in the mirror, something we might want to do periodically to understand how we got where we are today in our present life. The mistakes and triumphs of our past affect our future. Remember that karma is the perfect balancing technique in the cosmos, giving us opportunities to face the challenges of our extended life path until we reach understanding and make spiritual progress that advances us. It is that way with everyone. We can become agents of real change in our lives and our world. Understanding the result of our choices is the key.

⟿ Exercise: Visit Yourself in the Future

What's Needed

- a secluded, quiet place to meditate without interruption
- loose-fitting, comfortable clothing with shoes, jewelry, and other external items removed
- a mat or blanket to recline on your back or else a straight-backed chair

Procedure

Admittedly, this exercise to visit yourself in the future will prove most difficult for many people, but you might find it easier every time you try it. The reason that it might seem difficult is because you have very little frame of reference at hand for picturing yourself in the future. You do, however, carry with you your hopes and dreams that you want to access for this to be a successful exercise. You need to let the picture of those hopes and dreams fill in for you without attempting to steer the direction of things.

First, recline on your back with arms and legs outstretched or sit erect in the chair with feet firmly planted for grounding and no parts of your body crossed.

Focus on putting your physical body to sleep, beginning with your feet and working your way up to the top of your head, until your body is resting peacefully and your heightened consciousness is operating without obstruction.

Begin deep, rhythmic breathing and continue this pattern, conscious of the energy in the air, holding it inside you with your blessing, and then returning it to the world with your thanks.

Consciously access the energy centers of your subtle outer bodies from the base of your spine to the top of your head, visualizing the magical properties of the red, orange, yellow, green, blue, indigo, and violet flames that burn within you at your disposal.

Tune out all external and internal distractions until you reach a still point deep within and you see only a blank slate with your mind's eye.

On this slate, focus on seeing a vision of your future self. You could summon a picture of yourself at a later age in this lifetime or even in a future life incarnation. Request access to this vision and patiently wait for a picture to form. Spirit will supply it, for it is your eternal connection between what we commonly call the past, present, and future. Trust your spirit connection to supply the picture for you. Wait until the picture forms in your mind's eye as you appear, the setting in which you appear, and the time of this part of your life.

When the picture has formed, trust it as a perfect road map and follow it to that place and time until you find the future you in that time and place. Take some time to adjust yourself and convince yourself that you are truly there, observing your future self.

You will not be observed, as you have no physical form in this time period, so you can study this future version of yourself unobserved. Take your time to determine whether this is an older version of your current life or a future life. You should be able to see a physical resemblance if this is just an older version of your current life. You will probably find it easier to relate to an older version of your current life, too. But in either case, you should be able to relate to yourself at any point along the timeline.

Try to read the thoughts of this person in front of you and notice their body language. Observe where this person lives, how this person dresses, and how this person acts. If there are other people present, notice how this future version of you relates to these other people.

If you feel that this future version of you lacks emotional, mental, or spiritual energy, you could project some of the energy that is lacking from the energy that you have brought with you with your subtle energy bodies. This person in front of you is still you, so there is no ethical or practical problem with boosting yourself at this point in your timeline, helping you to rejuvenate in this new setting.

When you sense that you have gained meaningful insight into your future destiny, return instantly to your physical body back in the meditation room by simply focusing your attention on that reclining body.

Take some time when you return to your body to reflect on what you have learned about your destiny. Do not return full sensation to your physical body and open your eyes until you have sorted out what insights you have gained.

You might jot down your observations in a notepad and reflect on how your current direction is leading you to this future situation. Is there something you need to adjust or correct in your life, based on these insights into the future?

⟶ Exercise: Looking into the Future of Your Community

What's Needed

- a secluded, quiet place for meditating without interruption
- comfortable, loose-fitting clothing with shoes, jewelry, and all external items removed
- a mat or blanket to recline on your back or else a straight-backed chair

Procedure

Like the last exercise, going to the future for insight into the destiny of your people is not easy, because you have little frame of reference or attachment to this future you haven't realized yet. You probably find it difficult to accept that you can perform this sort of vision quest. But rest assured that you have a natural karmic attraction to all aspects of yourself and can accurately track yourself anywhere and anytime.

Karma acts on a practical level like an electromagnet because you are connecting companion parts with the electromagnetic energy of your consciousness and your subtle energy bodies that correspond to all levels of reality. These are your people who you will be observing in the future, so you have a natural attachment to them.

Simply recline on your back on the mat with arms and legs outstretched or sit erect in the chair with your feet firmly planted for grounding.

Now focus on putting your physical body to sleep, beginning with your feet and working your way up to the top of your head until your body is resting peacefully and your heightened consciousness is operating without obstruction.

Begin deep, rhythmic breathing and continue this pattern, conscious of the energy in the air, holding it inside you with your blessing, and then returning it to the world with your thanks.

Consciously access the energy centers of your subtle outer bodies, from the base of your spine to the top of your head, visualizing the magical properties of the red, orange, yellow, green, blue, indigo, and violet flames that burn within you.

Tune out all external and internal distractions until you reach a still point deep within and see only a blank slate with your mind's eye.

Focus on seeing a vision of your future self; you can summon a picture of the people close to you in your community at a later date. You should envision them in the place where you now live, although the place might be somewhat different in the future. Request access to this vision and patiently wait for a picture to form. Spirit will supply it, your eternal connection between what we commonly call the past, present, and future. Trust your spirit connection to supply the picture for you. Wait until the picture forms in your mind's eye. This is your internal vision. See a picture forming on a screen before your mind's eye. Fill the picture with the people you want to visit, the place you want to go, the time of your visit, and what you want to learn there.

When the picture has formed, trust it as a perfect road map and follow it to that place and time until you find your community there. Take some time to adjust yourself and convince yourself that you are truly there, observing your community as they have advanced and the world around you has changed.

You will not be observed because you have no physical form. Consequently, you can study this future version of your community unobserved. Be a perfect witness to what you see with your new eyes and new ears in your heightened state of consciousness. Take it all in and sense what the people think and feel in this future world. Notice how your world has changed.

When you sense that you have gained some insight into the future, shift your focus back to your reclining physical body to return to the meditation room.

Allow yourself time to sort through what you have witnessed before fully restoring sensation to your body and opening your eyes. Meditate on what you have learned and reflect on it.

This is similar to what shamans do in a vision quest or spirit walking to bring insights to their tribe. What have you learned? What corrections should be considered to bring about a better future? What things should be avoided?

You have gained insights that may guide you to a better future. Your vision of the future indicates how your current course of action and that of your community is leading you to a certain version of the future. You can correct this course by changing your energy day by day. You can become an agent of change in your life and in your world.

Afterword

I recognize that some readers without personal experience of time shifts might find it difficult to relate to some of the stories and observations in this book. I cannot attest to the accuracy of all of the stories I've included but have tried to verify all first-person accounts and carefully check all of the subjects that I interviewed. Other classic stories are included; however, there was no way to validate them other than to double-check the reports with various sources. While these stories might appear to be urban legends of dubious reliability, I would suggest that anecdotal evidence, at best, offers a pattern to review. It's totally up to you to decide whether these stories ring true for you.

Slips in time are something that many people may find hard to discuss on a personal level. On the other hand, you might be surprised by the response you get if you broach this subject with friends. It's likely that several of them have experienced sudden shifts in time or know others who have.

However, given that we have no real understanding of the phenomenon, we cannot deal with it without feeling a little awkward. Additionally, we have no frame of reference for such momentary divergence into what seems to be a parallel or non-ordinary reality. We are convinced that our previous experiences of what we call "now" is the only "now" that we can experience. Consequently, we might believe that other instances on our continuous timeline are dead moments of the past or the impossibly distant future. If you try the exercises in this book, though, they might help you to become comfortable with the concept of alternate realities.

I do think it's important to recognize that our physical world is alive with potential and not fully formed, awaiting our conscious attention to apply the finishing touches. The moving carpet on which we live can move with the speed of light and take us for quite a ride in many directions to explore various windows of exploration.

My only other comment is to extend a sincere thanks to explorer and author Frank Joseph for his encouragement when I was ready to abandon this project midstream. I was surprised to find that Frank has personal experience with time shifts. You just never know about some people and where they have traveled until you ask.

VON BRASCHLER

Bibliography

Amao, Albert Soria. *Awaken the Power Within: In Defense of Self-Help.* New York: TarcherPerigee, 2018.

Anastopoulos, Charis. *Particle or Wave: The Evolution of the Concept of Matter in Modern Physics.* Princeton, N.J.: Princeton University Press, 2008.

Arkani-Hamed, Nima, Savas Dimopoulous, and Georgi Dvali. "The Universe's Unseen Dimensions." *Scientific American,* August 2000.

Arntz, William, Betty Chasse, and Mark Vicente. *What the Bleep Do We Know?* DVD, Los Angeles, Calif.: 20th Century Fox, 2005.

Aurobindo, Sri. *The Secret of the Veda.* Pondicherry, India: Sri Aurobindo Ashram Publication, 1971.

Backster, Cleve. *Primary Perception: Biocommunication with Plants, Living Foods, and Human Cells.* Anza, Calif.: White Rose Millennium Press, 2003.

Bailey, Alice. *The Light of the Soul.* New York: Lucis Publishing Company, 1955.
———. *A Treatise on White Magic.* New York: Lucis Publishing Company, 1998.

Barbour, Julian. *The End of Time: The Next Revolution in Physics.* New York: Oxford University Press, 2001.

Bartusiak, Marcia. *Einstein's Unfinished Symphony: Listening to the Sounds of Space-Time.* New York: Berkley Books, 2003.

Bell, Madison Smartt. *Lavoisier in the Year One: The Birth of a New Science in an Age of Revolution.* New York: W. W. Norton & Co., 2006.

Bentov, Itzhak. *Stalking the Wild Pendulum: On the Mechanics of Consciousness.* Rochester, Vt.: Destiny Books, 1998.

Besant, Annie. *The Bhagavad Gita: The Lord's Song.* Adyar, India: The Theosophical Publishing House, 1953.

———. *Thought Power: In Control and Culture.* Wheaton, Ill.: Quest Books, 1967.

Besant, Annie, and Charles W. Leadbeater. *Thought-Forms.* Adyar, India: Theosophical Publishing Society, 1901.

Blavatsky, Helena P. *Collected Writings.* Adyar, India: Theosophical Publishing House, 1966.

———. *The Secret Doctrine.* Adyar, India: Theosophical Society, 1986.

———. *The Voice of the Silence: Chosen Fragments from the Book of the Golden Precepts.* Chicago: Theosophy Company, 1928.

Bowman, Carol. *Children's Past Lives: How Past Memories Affect Your Child.* New York: Bantam, 1998.

Braschler, Von. *Confessions of a Reluctant Ghost Hunter.* Rochester, Vt.: Destiny Books, 2014.

———. *Conversations with the Dream Mentor.* St. Paul, Minn.: Llewellyn Publications, 2003.

———. *Moving in the Light.* Pine Mountain Club, Calif: Shanti Publishing, 2018.

———. *Perfect Timing.* St. Paul, Minn.: Llewellyn Publications, 2002.

———. *Seven Secrets of Time Travel.* Rochester, Vt.: Destiny Books, 2012.

Brennan, Barbara Ann. *Hands of Light: A Guide to Healing through the Human Energy Field.* New York: Bantam Doubleday Dell, 1988.

Bryant, Edwin F. *The Yoga Sutras of Patanjali.* New York: North Point Press, 2009.

Campbell, Don. *The Roar of Silence: Healing Powers of Breath, Tone & Chant.* Wheaton, Ill.: Theosophical Publishing House, 1989.

Castaneda, Carlos. *Journey to Ixtland.* New York: Washington Square Press, 1991.

———. *A Separate Reality.* New York: Pocket Books, 1991.

———. *Tales of Power.* New York: Pocket Books, 1991.

Cooper, Callum E. *Telephone Calls from the Dead.* Hampshire, UK: Tricorn Books, 2013.

Dash, Mike. "When Three British Boys Traveled to Medieval England (Or Did They?)." *Smithsonian,* July 21, 2011.

Devi, Parama Karuna. *Bhagavata Purana.* CreateSpace Independent Publishing Platform, 2017.

Dossey, Larry. *Healing Words: The Power of Prayer and the Practice of Medicine.* New York: HarperCollins, 1993.

Dushkova, Zinovia. *The Secret Book of Dzyan: Unveiling the Hidden Truth about the Oldest Manuscript in the World and its Divine Authors.* Regina, Saskatchewan: Radiant Books, 2018.

Einstein, Albert. *The Theory of Relativity & Other Essays.* New York: MJF Books, 1955.

Emoto, Massaro. *The Hidden Messages in Water.* New York: Atria Books, 2005.

———. *Messages from Water and the Universe.* Carlsbad, Calif.: Hay House, 2010.

———. *The Miracle of Water.* New York: Atria Books, 2007.

Finney, Jack. "I'm Scared." *Collier's,* September 15, 1951.

Gawain, Shakti. *Creative Visualization.* Novato, Calif.: New World Library, 1978.

Gittner, Louis. *Listen, Listen, Listen.* Eastsound, Wash.: Louis Foundation Publishers, 1980.

———. *Love Is a Verb.* Eastsound, Wash.: Touch the Heart Press, 1987.

Goddard, Victor. *Flight Towards Reality.* London: Turnstone Books, 1975.

Godwin, Joscelyn. *Harmonies of Heaven and Earth: The Spiritual Dimensions of Music.* Rochester, Vt.: Inner Traditions, 1987.

Goet, J. Richard. *Time Travel in Einstein's Universe: The Physical Possibilities of Travel through Time.* New York: Mariner Books, 2002.

Heline, Corinne. *The Esoteric Music of Richard Wagner.* La Canada, Calif.: New Age Press, 1974.

Henley, William Ernest. *Poems by William Ernest Henley.* London: Forgotten Books, 2012.

Hirshfield, Alan. *The Electric Life of Michael Faraday.* New York: Walker & Company, 2006.

Homer. *Iliad.* Translated by Robert Fagles. New York: Penguin Classics, 1998.

———. *Odyssey.* Translated by Robert Fagles. New York: Penguin Classics, 1999.

Joseph, Frank. *Power Place and the Master Builders of Antiquity: Unexplained Mysteries of the Past.* Rochester, Vt.: Bear & Company, 2018.

———. *Synchronicity as Mystical Experience: Applying Meaning Coincidence in Your Life.* Pine Mountain Club, Calif.: Ancient Mysteries, Shanti Publishing, 2018.

———. *Synchronicity & You: Understand the Role of Meaningful Coincidence in Your Life.* Rockport, Mass.: Element Books Ltd., 1999.

Jourdain, Eleanor, and Charlotte Moberly. *An Adventure.* Independently published, 2016.

Karagulla, Shafica, and Dora Van Gelder Kunz. *The Chakras and the Human Energy Fields* Wheaton, Ill.: Theosophical Publishing House, 1998.

King, Serge Kahili. *Imagineering for Health.* Wheaton, Ill.: Quest Books. 1987.

Krishnamurti, Jiddu. *At the Feet of the Master.* Morrisville, N.C.: Lulu.com, 2018.

Krishnamurti, Jiddu. *Commentaries on Living.* Wheaton, Ill.: Theosophical Publishing House, 1995.

Leadbeater, Charles W. *The Chakras.* Wheaton, Ill.: Theosophical Publishing House, 1997.

———. *Telepathy: The 'Respectable' Phenomenon.* New York: Macmillan Book Club Edition, 1971.

Lingerman, Hal. *The Healing Energies of Music.* Wheaton, Ill.: Theosophical Publishing House, 1995.

MacIsaac, Tara. "Accounts of People Who Seem to Literally Be from Parallel Universes." *The Epoch Times,* May 6, 2016.

———. "Famous Time Slips: Urban Legends or Portals to the Past?" *The Epoch Times,* Aug. 8, 2014.

Maharishi Mahesh Yogi. *Science of Being and the Art of Living: Transcendental Meditation.* New York: Plume re-issue edition, 2001.

Massey, Gerald. *The Natural Genesis.* Baltimore: Black Classic Press, 1998.

McKenzie, Andrew. *Adventures in Time: Encounters with the Past.* London: Athlone Press, 1997.

McLuhan, Marshall, and Quentin Fiore. *The Medium Is the Message.* New York: Random House, 1967.

Merleau-Ponty, Maurice. *Phenomenology of Perception.* Translated by Colin Smith. London: Rutledge & Kegan, 1962.

Milton, John. *Paradise Lost.* New York: Penguin Classics, 2003.

Nagy, Andras M. *The Secrets of Pythagoras.* Charleston, S.C: CreateSpace Independent Publishing Platform, 2007.

Narby, Jeremy. *Intelligence in Nature: An Inquiry into Knowledge.* New York: Jeremy Tarcher, 2005.

Newton, Michael. *Journey of Souls.* St. Paul, Minn.: Llewellyn Publications, 1999.

Offutt, Jason. *What Lurks Beyond: The Paranormal in Your Back Yard.* Kirksville, Mo.: Truman State University Press, 2010.

Olcott, Henry Steele. *Old Diary Leaves.* Wheaton, Ill.: Theosophical Publishing House, 1975.

Ostrander, Sheila, Lynn Shroeder, and Ivan T. Sanderson. *Psychic Discoveries behind the Iron Curtain*. New York: Bantam Books, 1971.

Ouspensky, P. D. *In Search of the Miraculous*. New York: Mariner Books, 2001.

———. *Tertiam Origanum*. Kila, Mont.: Kessinger Publishing Company, 1998.

Paulson, Genevieve Lewis. *Energy Focused Meditation*. St. Paul, Minn.: Llewellyn Publishing Company, 1997.

Pierrakos, John. *Core Energetics*. Mendocino, Calif.: Evolution Publishing, 2005.

Plato. *Complete Words by Plato*. Indianapolis, Ind.: Hackett Publishing Company, 1997.

Radha, Swami Sivananda. *Light & Vibration: Consciousness, Mysticism & the Culmination of Yoga*. Kootenay, BC: Timeless Books, 2007.

Ritkin, Jeremy. *Entropy: Into the Greenhouse World*. New York: Bantam Books, 1989.

Roberts, Jane. *Seth Speaks: The Eternal Validity of the Soul*. Novato, Calif.: Amber-Allen Pub., New World Library, 1994.

Satchedananda, Sri S. *The Yoga Sutras of Pantanjali*. Buckingham, Va.: Integral Yoga Distribution, 1990.

Skolimowski. Henryk. *Theatre of the Mind*. Wheaton, Ill.: Quest Books, 1984.

Smith, Ingram. *Truth Is a Pathless Land: A Journey with Krishnamurti*. Wheaton, Ill.: Quest Books, 1989.

Sedgwick, Icy. "Time Slips: Urban Legend, Ghost Story, or Utter Nonsense?" *Icy Sedgwick*, www.icysedgwick.com/time-slips. September 14, 2019.

Smith, Penelope. *Animal Talk: Interspecies Telepathic Communication*. Point Reyes Station, Calif.: Pegasus Publications, 1996.

———. *Animals . . . Our Return to Wholeness*. Point Reyes Station, Calif.: Pegasus Publications, 1993.

Steiger, Brad. *One with the Light: Authentic Near-Death Experience that Changed Lives and Revealed the Beyond*. New York: Signet, 1994.

———. *Words from the Source*. New York: Prentice-Hall, 1975.

Stevenson, Ian. *Children Who Remember Previous Lives*. Jefferson, N.C.: McFarland, 2000.

Stone, Robert B. *The Secret Life of Your Cells*. Atglen, Penn.: Schiffer Pub. Ltd., 1997.

Strager, Hanne, and Sarah Darwin. *A Modest Genius: The Story of Darwin's Life and How His Ideas Changed Everything*. CreateSpace Independent Publishing Platform, 2016.

Telang, Vensa, and Kashinath Trimbak Telang. *Bhagavad Gita.* Overland Park, Kans.: Digireads.com Publishing, 2017.

Thompkins, Peter, and Christopher Bird. *The Secret Life of Plants.* New York: Harper & Row Publishers, Inc., 1989.

———. *Secrets of the Soil.* Anchorage, Alas.: Earthpulse Incorporated, 1998.

Vance, Bruce *A. DreamScape: Voyage in an Alternate Reality.* Wheaton, Ill.: Quest Books, 1995.

———. *MindScape: Exploring the Reality of Thought Forms.* Wheaton, Ill.: Quest Books, 1995.

Wagner, Stephen. "Time Travelers: Journeys into the Past and Future." *LiveAbout* website, August 14, 2018.

Webster, Richard. *Aura Reading for Beginners.* St. Paul, Minn.: Llewellyn Publications, 1998.

Weschcke, Carl, and Joe Slate. *Self-Empowerment and the Subconscious.* Woodbury, Minn.: Llewellyn Publications, 2018.

Wood, Ernest. *The Seven Rays.* Wheaton, Ill.: Theosophical Publishing House, 1972.

Index

About the Author

Von Braschler is the author of several books on consciousness expansion and time. He has led workshops throughout the United States and the United Kingdom and has appeared on countless radio and television shows. He has also served as a faculty member at Omega Institute in New York and formerly hosted a popular podcast, "Healing with your Pets: Our Psychic, Spiritual Connection," which was rebroadcast in various places worldwide.

He has worked as an award-winning journalist in the newspaper and magazine field and has worked at various book publishing houses as well.

Braschler is a lifetime member of the international Theosophical Society, which has its headquarters in Adyar, India.

He splits his time between Minnesota and a small island in the state of Washington where he spends his spare time taking pictures, hiking, sailing, feeding birds, and caring for animals. His cat inspects all work before it leaves his desk. If there is something amiss here, blame the cat.

Books of Related Interest

Seven Secrets of Time Travel
Mystic Voyages of the Energy Body
by Von Braschler
Foreword by Frank Joseph

Confessions of a Reluctant Ghost Hunter
A Cautionary Tale of Encounters with Malevolent Entities
and Other Disembodied Spirits
by Von Braschler

Living Souls in the Spirit Dimension
The Afterlife and Transdimensional Reality
by Chris H. Hardy, Ph.D.

Transcending the Speed of Light
Consciousness, Quantum Physics, and the Fifth Dimension
by Marc Seifer, Ph.D.

The Immortal Mind
Science and the Continuity of Consciousness beyond the Brain
by Ervin Laszlo
with Anthony Peake

The Akashic Experience
Science and the Cosmic Memory Field
by Ervin Laszlo

Precognitive Dreamwork and the Long Self
Interpreting Messages from Your Future
by Eric Wargo

Morphic Resonance
The Nature of Formative Causation
by Rupert Sheldrake

INNER TRADITIONS • BEAR & COMPANY
P.O. Box 388
Rochester, VT 05767
1-800-246-8648
www.InnerTraditions.com

Or contact your local bookseller